PROJECT 27/28

An Enquiry into
quality of care
and its effect
on the survival
of babies born
at 27–28 weeks

Edited by
Mary Macintosh
Director, CESDI

London: TSO

Published by TSO (The Stationery Office) and available from:

Online
www.tso.co.uk/bookshop

Mail, Telephone, Fax & E-mail
TSO
PO Box 29, Norwich, NR3 1GN
Telephone orders/General enquiries: 0870 600 5522
Fax orders: 0870 600 5533
E-mail: book.orders@tso.co.uk
Textphone 0870 240 3701

TSO Shops
123 Kingsway, London, WC2B 6PQ
020 7242 6393 Fax 020 7242 6394
68-69 Bull Street, Birmingham B4 6AD
0121 236 9696 Fax 0121 236 9699
9-21 Princess Street, Manchester M60 8AS
0161 834 7201 Fax 0161 833 0634
16 Arthur Street, Belfast BT1 4GD
028 9023 8451 Fax 028 9023 5401
18-19 High Street, Cardiff CF10 1PT
029 2039 5548 Fax 029 2038 4347
71 Lothian Road, Edinburgh EH3 9AZ
0870 606 5566 Fax 0870 606 5588

TSO Accredited Agents
(see Yellow Pages)

and through good booksellers

Applications for reproduction should be made in writing to:
CEMACH
Chiltern Court
188 Baker Street
London
NW1 5SD
www.cemach.org.uk

Photograph supplied courtesy of BLISS – the premature baby charity

First published 2003

ISBN 0 11 703089 9

Printed in the United Kingdom for The Stationery Office
134598 C15 03/03 5673

Contents

Foreword   v

Acknowledgements   vii

1   Introduction   1

2   Mothers and babies   9

3   Fetal well-being – assessment prior to labour   25

4   Antenatal management of preterm delivery   33

5   Intrapartum care   45

6   Neonatal resuscitation   61

7   Early thermal care   73

8   Surfactant therapy   81

9   Ventilatory support   89

10   Cardiovascular support   95

11   Management of infection   103

12   Organisation of care   111

13   Transfers before and after delivery   119

14   Perinatal pathology   131

15   Communication and record-keeping   139

16   Panel conclusions – overall grade of care   147

17   Lost in the figures   153

Appendix

     Abbreviations   161

     Glossary   163

     Project 27/28 standards   171

     References   173

Foreword

The publication of this report comes at an important time in the continuing development of the Confidential Enquiry into Stillbirths and Deaths in Infancy (CESDI). For the last 7 years the Enquiry has been the responsibility of the Maternal and Child Health Research Consortium overseen by representatives of the Royal Colleges of Midwives, Obstetricians and Gynaecologists, Paediatrics and Child Health, and Pathologists. The Consortium has had excellent individuals working at the Secretariat, an extensive and enthusiastic network of Regional Co-ordinators and collaborators, and a multidisciplinary Professional Advisory/Steering Group. All have contributed to the development, review and analysis of this unique Enquiry report: unique in that it is the first report from the UK Confidential Enquiries which has utilised a case control approach, collection of denominator data for the prescribed area of enquiry (births at 27–28 weeks gestation), specially developed enquiry data forms, and evaluation by multidisciplinary enquiry panels against specifically developed panel questions assessing care against predetermined standards. This methodology, which has been refined further for ongoing enquiry areas, has produced robust data and makes compelling reading. It demonstrates the surprisingly high levels of survival that can now be achieved by good antenatal and post delivery care, with assessment and appropriate transfer to units which have the necessary neonatal facilities, and continuing improvements occurring within neonatal intensive care. In general care is good, but the recommendation sections of the report highlight areas for potential improvement that might further improve the chances not only of survival but of survival with reduced potential for morbidity and handicap.

This report and its recommendations should provide the basis for intensive local discussion and review of protocols and care facilities in all obstetric and neonatal units. Purchasers of maternity care should be aware of its recommendations.

From 1 April 2003, the continuing responsibility of the Enquiry will pass to the newly formed Confidential Enquiry into Maternal and Child Health (CEMACH). We trust that they will continue to develop the enquiry process along the lines as developed by CESDI, to help further develop understanding into the causes of stillbirth and neonatal deaths and improve care for all pregnant women and their children.

Professor Robert W. Shaw CBE

Chair, Maternal and Child Health Research Consortium

Acknowledgements

Maternal and Child Health Research Consortium (MCHRC) Executive Steering Group

Professor Robert Shaw (Chair)	Royal College of Obstetricians and Gynaecologists
Ms Polly Ferguson	Royal College of Midwives
Dr Steve Gould	Royal College of Pathologists
Dr Patricia Hamilton	Royal College of Paediatrics and Child Health

Interim Advisory Group

Professor Andrew Wilkinson (Chair)	Professor of Paediatrics, University of Oxford
Mrs Vicky Bailey	Senior Midwife, Nottingham Health Authority
Miss Sue Burr	Adviser on Paediatric Nursing, Royal College of Nursing
Dr Patrick Cartlidge	Consultant Neonatal Paediatrician, University of Wales College of Medicine
Dr Jean Chapple	Consultant Perinatal Epidemiologist, Westminster Primary Care Trust
Mr Jim Dornan	Consultant Obstetrician, Royal Maternity Hospital, Belfast
Mr Keith Greene	Consultant Obstetrician and Gynaecologist, Derriford Hospital, Plymouth
Ms Patricia Hanson	CESDI Regional Co-ordinator, South East Thames
Mrs Eileen Hutton	parental voice
Dr Jean Keeling	Consultant Paediatric Pathologist, Royal Hospital for Sick Children, Edinburgh
Dr Mark Lambert	Consultant in Public Health Medicine, Gateshead and South Tyneside Health Authority
Mrs Linda Lamont	parental voice
Mrs Stephanie Meakin	Practice Development Co-ordinator, Royal College of Midwives
Dr Gavin Young	General Practitioner, Temple Sowerby, Cumbria

CESDI secretariat

Dr Mary Macintosh	Director
Mrs Mary Humphreys	Personal Assistant to Director
Ms Helen Pinfold	Project Manager (to April 2002)
Mrs Helen Frost	Project Manager (from April 2002)
Dr Jo Modder	Clinical Co-ordinator – Obstetrics
Dr Marilena Korkodilos	Clinical Co-ordinator – Paediatrics (until February 2002)
Dr Dominique Acolet	Clinical Co-ordinator – Paediatrics (from April 2002)
Mrs Allyson Williams	Midwife
Mr Charles Lee	IT Specialist
Ms Shamina Rahman	Information Manager

CESDI regional co-ordinators

Northern	Ms Marjorie Renwick
Yorkshire	Ms Lesley Anson
Trent	Ms Sue Wood
East Anglia	Ms Carol Hay
North West Thames	Ms Stephanie Roberts
North East Thames	Ms Shona Golightly, Ms Joan Noble
South East Thames	Ms Patricia Hanson
South Thames West	Mrs Alison Miller
Wessex	Ms Melanie Gompels
Oxford	Mrs Heather Kirlow
South Western	Ms Rosie Thompson
West Midlands	Ms Donna Drinkall, Ms Pat McGeown
Mersey	Ms Julie Maddocks
North Western	Dr Jean Sands
Wales	Ms Jane Stewart
Northern Ireland	Ms Terry Falconer, Dr Maureen Scott

Project 27/28 Working Group

*denotes section lead for the Recommendations Advisory Group

Dr Patrick Cartlidge	Consultant Neonatal Paediatrician, University of Wales College of Medicine
Ms Julia Chachere	CESDI Regional Co-ordinator, London
Professor Mike Clarke	Professor of Epidemiology, University of Leicester
Professor Kate Costeloe*	Professor of Paediatrics, Homerton and Royal London Hospitals, London
Mrs Elizabeth Draper	Deputy Director of Trent Infant Mortality and Morbidity Study, and Senior Research Fellow, University of Leicester
Professor David Field*	Professor of Neonatal Medicine, Leicester Royal Infirmary, Leicester
Professor Peter Fleming*	Professor of Infant Health and Developmental Physiology, Royal Hospital for Sick Children, Bristol
Dr Alan Gibson	Consultant Neonatologist, Jessop Hospital for Women, Sheffield
Dr Steve Gould	Consultant Paediatric Pathologist, John Radcliffe Hospital, Oxford
Mrs Niki Jakeman	CESDI – Midwife
Dr Mike Lewins*	Consultant Paediatrician, Lincoln County Hospital, Lincoln
Dr Mary Macintosh	CESDI – Director
Ms Sara McCarthy	CESDI – Data Analyst
Professor Neil Marlow*	Professor of Neonatal Medicine, Queens Medical Centre, Nottingham
Mr Ralph Settatree*	Consultant Obstetrician, Birmingham Heartlands Hospital, Birmingham
Ms Jane Stewart	CESDI Regional Co-ordinator, Wales
Professor Jim Thornton	Reader in Obstetrics and Gynaecology, University of Nottingham
Professor Andrew Wilkinson*	Professor of Paediatrics, University of Oxford

Project 27/28 Recommendations Advisory Group

This group included the members of the Project 27/28 Working Group and in addition the following (* denotes section lead):

Ms Arona Ahmed	London
Ms Jane Baker	Royal College of Midwives, London
Dr Harry Baumer	Plymouth
Dr Jean Chapple*	London
Professor Richard Cooke*	Liverpool
Dr Phil Cox	Birmingham
Mr Jim Dornan*	Belfast
Dr Andy Ewer	Birmingham
Dr David Ferguson	Newport
Ms Lindsay Frank	London
Dr Alan Gibson	Sheffield
Dr Bryan Gill	Leeds
Ms Melissa Good	London
Ms Bonnie Green	BLISS
Dr Patricia Hamilton	London
Ms Claire Himbury	Canterbury
Dr Anita Holdcroft	London
Ms Angela Horsley	Canterbury
Mrs Eileen Hutton	parental voice, Interim Advisory Group
Ms Mervi Jokinen	Royal College of Midwives, London
Ms Sara Kent	Northampton
Mrs Linda Lamont	parental voice, Interim Advisory Group
Mrs Lucy Lelliott	SANDS
Dr Andrew Long	Orpington
Dr Sheila Macphail*	Newcastle
Ms Shanit Marshall	BLISS
Dr Anne May	Leicester
Ms Stephanie Michaelides	London
Mrs Joan Oliver	Ashington

Ms Caroline Pepys	Oxford
Ms Tina Pollard	Northampton
Ms Stephanie Roberts	London
Dr David Schapira	Winchester
Professor Robert Shaw*	University of Nottingham
Mr Andrew Shennan*	London
Dr Aung Soe	Gillingham
Ms Rosie Thompson	Bristol
Ms Tracey Thrift	Lincolnshire
Mr Derek Tuffnell*	Bradford
Mrs Sue Wood	Sheffield

Authors of the report

This report brings together several years of work by numerous contributors both inside and outside the CESDI organization. For the writing of this report special thanks go to the following:

- Dominique Acolet and Marilena Korkodilos for their contribution to the neonatal sections
- Jo Modder for her contribution to the obstetric sections
- Phil Cox, Steve Gould and Dominique Acolet for the pathology chapter
- Jane Stewart and Allyson Williams for their contribution to the communication chapter
- Melanie Gompels and Allyson Williams for the 'Lost in the figures' chapter
- Jean Chapple for her advice on demographics
- Anita Holdcroft and Anne May for their advice on the anaesthetic section
- Jo Haviland for statistical advice throughout the project
- Charles Lee for preparation of figures and tables
- Members of the Interim Advisory Group, the Recommendation Advisory Group section leads, Dr Cliff Roberton and Professor Tim Chard who reviewed and commented on draft versions of the report.

In addition to the people named above, we would also like to acknowledge the considerable contribution of the support staff at the regional offices, the panellists, the many district co-ordinators and others based throughout England, Wales and Northern Ireland, who, often without recognition and in their own time, undertake work for CESDI.

Mary Macintosh, Director, CESDI

February 2003

Introduction

BACKGROUND

Prematurity is the major cause of neonatal deaths and as such was chosen in 1997 to be the focus for the national Confidential Enquiry into Stillbirth and Infant Deaths (CESDI) programme.

Prematurity refers to all live births prior to 37 weeks gestation and accounts for 13% of registrable births (All Wales Perinatal Survey, 1999) and 47% of neonatal deaths (CESDI 8th Annual Report, 2001). In 1997 survival rates were less than 5% at 24 weeks and rose to nearly 100% at 36 weeks (All Wales Perinatal Survey, 1997). The survival rate improved very rapidly between 24 and 28 weeks and by 28 weeks most babies were expected to survive. The scope of the national Enquiry programme was therefore focused on the care occurring at 27^{+0}–28^{+6} weeks gestation, hence the title 'Project 27/28'.

Project 27/28 included four initiatives to strengthen the evidence base for the recommendations from the findings. These were:

- the collection of denominator data
- provision of pre-specified standards
- a case control approach with enquiries into survivors
- a consultation process to underpin the recommendations.

CESDI – THE ORGANISATION

CESDI was established in 1992 to improve understanding of how the risks of death in late fetal life and infancy, from 20 weeks of pregnancy to 1 year after birth, might be reduced. It aims to identify patterns of practice or service provision that may be related to these deaths and from these make recommendations to improve future practice. CESDI receives 10 000 notifications annually via its own reporting system in England, Wales and

Northern Ireland. Enquiries are held on a subset of these with a focus on a specific topic.

In 1991 the Department of Health directed that the 14 health service regions of England should undertake perinatal mortality surveys. CESDI was subsequently organised on this regional basis, with separate arrangements for Wales and Northern Ireland. Each regional survey was established autonomously and has a full-time co-ordinator together with varying numbers of support staff. There is a central secretariat based in London. This was the arrangement between 1992 and 2003, during the running of Project 27/28. There have been several changes of regional boundaries since 1992 but CESDI has retained its original regional structure and the term region in this report refers to the original CESDI regions.

CESDI was initially funded directly by the Department of Health and supervised by a National Advisory Body. In April 1996 the Maternal and Child Health Research Consortium (MCHRC) assumed responsibility for the management of CESDI. The Consortium comprises representatives from the Royal College of Obstetricians and Gynaecologists, the Royal College of Paediatrics and Child Health, the Royal College of Pathology and the Royal College of Midwives. The MCHRC oversees the running of the Enquiry.

In 1999 CESDI with three other National Enquiries came under the umbrella of the National Institute for Clinical Excellence (NICE). A review of the Enquiries recommended that CESDI should join with the Confidential Enquiry into Maternal Deaths to form the Confidential Enquiry into Maternal and Child Health. This has a wider brief and includes children up to the age of 16 years. This change will occur in April 2003.

ENQUIRY APPROACH

Unique to CESDI is the use of multidisciplinary panels held at regional level. The assessors are selected locally and are independent of the case and the relevant hospital. The assessors are provided with the anonymised medical record before the panel, and meet to discuss between four and six cases. The objective of the panel is to identify areas of suboptimal care and provide an overall assessment of the quality of care. After the Enquiry there is no direct feedback to individuals or to the unit concerned but the findings are recorded and aggregated centrally into a report.

THE AIM OF PROJECT 27/28

The aim of Project 27/28 was to identify patterns of practice or service provision that might contribute to the deaths of premature babies at 27–28 weeks gestation and from these to make recommendations for future practice. To achieve this aim there were two separate data collections based on:

1 The identification and outcome on the 28th day after delivery of all babies born alive in England, Wales and Northern Ireland between 27 and 28 weeks gestation over a 2-year period. This provided national and regional survival figures to day 28. The findings have been published in the 8th Annual Report (CESDI, 2001).

2 The undertaking of a Confidential Enquiry on all neonatal deaths and an equivalent number of the survivors in this gestational range. The scope of the Enquiry was the care given in pregnancy and up to the first 7 days of life. A summary and comparison of the Enquiry findings form the basis of this report.

DENOMINATOR – ALL BABIES BORN AT 27–28 WEEKS

Data on gestational age is not routinely collected on all births in England and Northern Ireland. This precludes the provision of national survival rates and trends for preterm babies. Much information comes from hospital-based studies and from population registers available in some English regions (e.g. Trent) and in Wales and Scotland. Extrapolation to a general population from a hospital-based study is limited as the studies are frequently based on small numbers and depend on the case mix. The population-based registers reflect the outcome for the individual region.

One of the aims of Project 27/28 was to provide national and regional survival figures to day 28.

Specially designed logbooks were introduced into all labour wards and neonatal units in England, Wales and Northern Ireland. All live-born babies with a clinical gestation between 26^{+0} and 29^{+6} weeks born between 1 September 1998 and 31 August 2000 were entered into the log by the CESDI Hospital Co-ordinator. The 4-week range was chosen to allow for inaccuracies in estimation of clinical gestation at birth. A minimum dataset was recorded on every baby entered in the log. The various locations for the baby in the first 28 days following birth were noted. Notification from the logs was sent from hospitals to the 16 regional co-ordinators and then to the central secretariat on a monthly basis. There were 3522 babies born at 27–28 weeks gestation in the 2-year period, and the overall survival rate to day 28 for this cohort was 88%, considerably better than anticipated at the outset of the project.

A full description of the denominator is given in the CESDI 8th Annual Report (2001).

PROJECT 27/28 – SUBJECTS FOR ENQUIRY

Criteria for Enquiry

The criteria for the Enquiry included:

- all neonatal deaths (i.e. deaths within the first 28 days)
- an equivalent number of babies who had survived to day 28.

Thirty-five babies with life-threatening malformations were excluded from the Enquiry. This was because the care given to this group of babies would be determined by their condition and not be representative of a baby born without complications at this gestation.

At the outset it had been planned to restrict enquiries to early neonatal deaths (first week of life). However, because of the unexpectedly high survival rates noted in the first 6 months of data collection, it was decided to extend the enquiries to include late neonatal deaths (up to 28 days).

Selection of controls

Controls were selected on a random basis from the cohort of babies known to have survived up to day 28.

Reference numbers for all babies recorded in the logbooks were held in a central database. The reference numbers of the babies who survived were categorised by gestation in completed weeks (27 and 28) and plurality (singleton and multiples). A computer programme then randomly selected from these categories to ensure that the proportion of babies within these categories was the same in the death and control groups.

THE ENQUIRY PANELS

Each panel comprised a number of regional assessors (range 3–18, median 8) from a wide range of expertise including obstetrics, neonatology, midwifery, neonatal nursing, pathology and public health. The assessors had not been involved with the care of the case and so were independent.

For each Enquiry the antenatal, delivery and neonatal medical records up to 7 days after delivery were anonymised by the regional co-ordinator. These were then sent to panel assessors with a structured enquiry form and a standards document (Appendix) for completion before the panel assessment. The medical record provided to the obstetricians and midwives was restricted to the care up to the point of delivery. This was to enable the assessment of this part of care to be made by assessors 'blind' to the outcome for the baby. Blinding was not feasible for the assessment of care after the delivery of the baby.

During the first year of the study, the panel assessments were held on babies who were born within a given region. A review 9 months after the start of the enquiries revealed that many regions had difficulty finding an independent consultant neonatologist. To address this problem, deaths and controls born in the second year were allocated by the CESDI secretariat via a national pool for panel assessment out of the region of birth. Thus all babies selected for enquiry that were born between 1 September 1998 and 31 August 1999 were enquired within region, and babies born after this were enquired out of region.

THE ENQUIRY PROFORMA

The scope of the Enquiry included the care in pregnancy, delivery and up to the first 7 days of life. The information was collected using a semi-structured Enquiry proforma comprising four sections (obstetric, neonatal, pathology and general). Each section addressed specific questions. The topics are outlined in Table 1.1. The proforma was designed and agreed by the Project 27/28 Working Group (CESDI 6th Annual Report, 1999) and is available on the CESDI website (www.cesdi.org.uk).

The Panel assessors were also asked to provide grades relating to the overall care of obstetric and neonatology components individually.

STANDARDS FOR ENQUIRY

A standards document was introduced for the panel assessors, to act as guidance and thereby improve the consistency of the assessment process. It comprised one standard relating to obstetric care and nine standards for neonatal care (see Appendix). Not all topics had well-established evidence-based standards, and when these were absent then accepted best practice was used as the basis. The standards document was compiled by the Project 27/28 Working Group (CESDI 6th Annual Report, 1999).

Table 1.1 Specific topics addressed by the Enquiry

Predelivery
    Administration of steroids
    Management of chorioamnionitis
    In-utero transfers
    Fetal surveillance antenatally and in labour

Postdelivery
    Resuscitation
    Early thermal care
    Use of surfactants
    Ventilatory and cardiovascular support
    Management of infection
    Transfers in the first 7 days of life

Pathology
    Standard of postmortem report
    Personnel undertaking report
    Contribution of postmortem to modification of clinical assessment
    Neuropathological findings

General
    Communication with parents
    Communication between maternity and neonatal staff
    Participation in trials
    Record-keeping
    Deficiencies in organisation

ANALYSIS – THE CASE CONTROL APPROACH

The recommendations from enquiries are usually derived from observations made on deaths alone. Comparable information from survivors is generally not available. In Project 27/28 a control group was included to clarify the relationship between putative risk factors and the death of the baby. The case control approach had the objective of comparing a wide spectrum of clinical care factors in a group of babies who died with that in a group of babies who survived. Failure of care that is commoner in the babies who died would point towards areas where improvements might reduce future neonatal mortality rates.

Case control studies have some limitations, notably bias and confounding. These may be minimised, but cannot always be eliminated, by careful initial design. Specific problems encountered are described in each section of this report, but three general issues stood out:

- care often cannot be assessed from completely objective information

- awareness of outcome may affect the opinion of assessors

- differences observed may be due to factors other than care.

For example, administration of corticosteroids to the mother is not always possible in the event of a rapid delivery. It may therefore be difficult to judge the efforts made to achieve this aim. 'Effort' is very subjective, but both effort and achievement are important and are relevant to the Enquiry. Easily measurable outcomes that parallel the standards of care are often not available; this was especially so for assessment of ventilation and cardiovascular support in the neonate (Chapters 9 and 10).

In Project 27/28 the comparisons of neonatal care were particularly difficult because the babies who died were sicker at birth than the babies who survived. Thus any comparison of care may be influenced more by the state of the baby than by the care itself (Chapter 2). To address this, statistical adjustments were made and these results are reported as adjusted odds ratios. The same adjusting factors were applied throughout to each comparison of neonatal care. Although this provided consistency it was a simplistic statistical model and it remains difficult to be certain that all relevant factors were allowed for in any case control comparison.

In summary, the major problems of the enquiry process in Project 27/28 are the lack of objectivity for the neonatal assessments and the difficulties of adjusting for the condition of the baby at birth. Despite this, there is no doubt that the control group provided a more informed view of the standards of care for babies at this gestation than would have been the case without any element of control.

DERIVING THE RECOMMENDATIONS

In the past, recommendations stemming from the results of a CESDI Enquiry have been made by a small group of experts, initially the National Advisory Body and currently the Interim Advisory Group, the professional advisory group for CESDI. In recent years emphasis has been placed on recommendations which are evidence-based, national in scope, and with input from consumers. As a consequence, the process of recommendation development for Project 27/28 has involved a wider consultation of experts via the Recommendations Advisory Group together with use of the Delphi technique.

Not surprisingly, the wider consultation process generated a large number of potential recommendations. At one extreme these concerned what would be regarded as relatively simple topics, to be found in any textbook. At the other extreme they addressed complex or recondite procedures which, although estimable in themselves, would require a firmer evidence base before they can be recommended as part of routine practice. In developing the recommendations the Recommendations Advisory Group have exerted their best efforts to ensure that the recommendations relate to the actual findings of Project 27/28. Thus a simple and superficially familiar topic, such as administration of corticosteroids to the mother, is highlighted because the enquiries revealed failures of care in this area which were associated with an excess of deaths of these premature babies. By contrast, technology such as the use of Doppler ultrasound in preterm labour is not emphasised because the evidence for its use is insufficient, either from the present or other studies, to justify its universal use.

The recommendations have been divided into those that require to be addressed at national and commissioning level and those that can be addressed at Trust level.

Surprisingly, there were three pathological events that were not associated with death or survival: clinical chorioamnionitis, proteinuric pregnancy-induced hypertension and major placental bleeding or abruption (Table 2.9). However, there is a body of evidence that points towards perinatal infection as a potent cause of brain injury in the term infant. This includes a meta-analysis which found a 4.7-fold increased relative risk of cerebral palsy among full-term infants whose mothers had clinical chorioamnionitis (Wu and Colford, 2000). Similarly, cerebral palsy in premature infants is associated with the presence of chorioamnionitis and maternal antibiotic use (O'Shea et al., 1998). Thus, although clinical chorioamnionitis was not associated with death in this study, an association with long-term neurological disability is not precluded. The same argument might also apply to the other pathological conditions. A follow-up study of these babies would evaluate this possibility.

The characteristics of the mothers associated with an increased risk of preterm birth at 27–28 weeks gestation can be compared to those of the maternity population of England, Wales and Northern Ireland. There were three notable differences: the proportion of multiple maternities, smokers and distribution of ethnicity.

One in four of maternities at 27–28 weeks was a multiple birth (CESDI 8th Annual Report, 2001) compared to 1 in 70 of all maternities (Chapple, 2001). Babies from multiple pregnancies are much more likely to be born early and are over seven times more likely to die in the first month of life than a singleton baby (Macfarlane and Mugford, 2000). Assisted reproductive techniques have played a large part in the recent rapid rise in the proportion of multiple pregnancies – from 11.6 multiple pregnancies per 1000 maternities in 1990 to 14.4 per 1000 in 1998 (Chapple, 2001). The Confidential Enquiries into Maternal Deaths in the UK 1997–99 (CEMD, 2001) suggests (although the numbers of deaths are very small) that multiple pregnancies may be harmful for mothers as well as babies, with a maternal mortality rate for mothers of twins being nearly twice that of mothers of singletons. It is therefore important for the chance of a multiple pregnancy with any assisted reproduction technique to be minimised.

In the enquiries 37% of all mothers smoked at some time during pregnancy, in contrast to 19% in the *Infant Feeding Survey 2000* (IFS, 2002). The latter were a representative sample of all maternities in the UK during the year 2000. The survey information was based on a questionnaire to the mother, whereas the Enquiry findings are based on the medical record.

This large difference highlights the significantly increased risk of preterm birth itself to women who smoke during pregnancy. There is ample evidence that interventions from professionals are more effective in stopping people smoking than smokers trying to stop by their own efforts alone. It is better to give advice than do nothing or to give self-help materials (Lancaster et al., 2000). However, in the group of mothers who delivered at 27–28 weeks gestation smoking per se was not associated with an increased mortality risk to the baby.

The ethnic origin of mothers in the Infant Feeding Survey (IFS, 2000) was recorded as 91% white, 3% Asian, 2% African, 1% mixed and <1% other. This compared to the Enquiry findings of 79% white, 9% African, 8% Asian, and 5% other. These data suggest that ethnic origin is important in the aetiology of preterm birth.

In contrast to the maternal characteristics, there were many differences between the two groups of babies. Babies who died were more likely to be male; to weigh less than the 5th centile; to have a non-lethal congenital abnormality; to have no heartbeat at delivery; to show poor respiratory effort at birth; and to be critically ill in the first 12 hours of life.

The underlying purpose of this report was to identify care factors that might be related to outcome. It is obviously highly important that these factors must be isolated from the condition of the baby: sicker babies are inevitably more at risk of a poor outcome regardless of the standard of care. Throughout this report an attempt has been made to eliminate the condition of the baby as a confounder by the use of adjusted odds ratios rather than crude odds ratios. This is a more accurate measure of the effect of care in its contribution to death.

A variety of measurements may be used to describe the condition of the baby within the first 12 hours of life. The two most familiar scoring systems are the Apgar score and the Clinical Risk Index for Babies (CRIB) score (International Neonatal Network, 1993). However, to adjust for any variable, its value needs to be recorded for each baby. Thus the quality of the data item sometimes limited the ability to adjust the analysis. For the purpose of this study it was decided to use the condition of 'absent or ineffective respiratory activity or persistent heart rate <100 beats/min at 5 minutes' (Table 6.1) as the variable that best described the condition of the baby at the time of birth.

SUMMARY

Most of the babies who died did so early on, with a quarter of deaths occurring within the first 24 hours and 70% within the first week of life. The babies who died were notably sicker at birth, and these findings imply that significant differences must exist antenatally. Despite this there were remarkably few maternal factors, either in background, past obstetric history or arising as a complication during the pregnancy, that differentiated between these mothers. This conundrum emphasises the difficulties for the health profession of identifying the mother at risk of losing her baby during the antenatal period. However, identifying the mother at risk for preterm birth appears to be an easier task, with the notably high prevalence of multiple pregnancy, smoking, history of previous preterm birth and non-white ethnic origin in these mothers.

RECOMMENDATIONS

At national and commissioning level

2.1 Funding and implementation of initiatives to help women and their families stop smoking in pregnancy and remain non-smokers should be continued.

At Trust level

2.2 Local champions should be appointed to coordinate services for pregnant women who want to give up smoking. This would include liaison with primary care teams to ensure appropriate referral to a dedicated person, providing a skilled intervention at an early stage, training midwives to provide brief interventions, liaison with Sure Start schemes to ensure joint effective working and providing supporting clinics or one-to-one support. *(http://www.doh.gov.uk/smokingprototypemay2002/pdfs/pregservs.pdf).*

Clinical practice

2.3 Clinicians should be aware that advice from doctors, structured interventions from midwives and nurses and individual and group counselling are effective interventions in helping women to stop smoking and should be included in their practice wherever possible (Lancaster et al., 2000).

2.4 Every effort should be made to avoid super-ovulation and multiple pregnancies when assisted reproductive techniques are used for subfertility and infertility.

3 Fetal well-being – assessment prior to labour

The aim of antenatal management is to identify the fetus at high risk of perinatal mortality or morbidity. The panels addressed the quality of care in assessment of the baby before the onset of labour by noting all fetal well-being assessments carried out after 20 weeks gestation and identifying any areas of concern. No standards were provided.

INVESTIGATIONS OF FETAL WELL-BEING

Most babies (80% or more) had an antenatal cardiotocograph (CTG), scan measurement after 20 weeks gestation and estimation of liquor volume (Table 3.1). Umbilical artery Doppler ultrasound scans and a full biophysical profile were undertaken in 36% and 12% respectively of the babies who survived and in 47% and 14% respectively of the babies who died (Table 3.1). Abnormalities of all types of tests were seen more frequently in the cases where the baby died (Table 3.2). The panels noted clinical suspicion that the fetus weighed less than the 5th centile in 16% of babies who survived and 32% of the babies who died.

PANEL OPINION

Panels addressed four questions:

- Was the assessment of fetal well-being adequate?
- Was the interpretation of the assessments adequate?
- Were the actions taken appropriate?
- Were the staff involved of appropriate seniority?

There was inadequate assessment of fetal well-being in 26% of babies who died and in 18% of babies who survived. This difference was significant (Table 3.3).

Table 3.1 Types of fetal well-being tests performed

	Babies who died (%) [a] n = 366	Babies who survived (%) [a] n = 395	Crude OR (95% CI) þ value
Antenatal CTG	288 (80.7)	334 (86.3)	0.66 (0.45–0.98) 0.04
[Data missing]	9	8	
Scan measurement >20 weeks	302 (83.4)	323 (83.7)	0.98 (0.67–1.44) 0.93
[Data missing]	4	9	
Liquor volume	282 (79.7)	305 (79.6)	1.00 (0.70–1.43) 0.99
[Data missing]	12	12	
Umbilical artery Dopplers	166 (46.8)	138 (36.0)	1.56 (1.16–2.09) 0.003
[Data missing]	11	12	
Full biophysical profile	48 (13.5)	44 (11.7)	1.18 (0.76–1.83) 0.46
[Data missing]	11	19	

[a] The percentage was calculated from the number of babies for which the information was provided.

Table 3.2 Abnormal results of fetal well-being tests

	Babies who died (%) [a]	Babies who survived (%) [a]	Crude OR (95% CI) þ value
Antenatal CTG	120/259 (46.3)	93/320 (29.1)	2.11 (1.49–2.97) <0.001
[Data missing]	19	14	
Scan measurement >20 weeks	116/290 (40)	69/316 (21.8)	2.39 (1.67–3.40) <0.001
[Data missing]	12	7	
Liquor volume	177/275 (64.4)	122/301 (40.5)	2.65 (1.89–3.71) <0.001
[Data missing]	7	4	
Umbilical artery Dopplers	92/161 (57.1)	54/135 (40)	2.00 (1.26–3.18) 0.003
[Data missing]	5	3	
Full biophysical profile	28/45 (62.2)	11/36 (30.6)	3.74 (1.48–9.49) 0.005
[Data missing]	3	8	
Predelivery evidence <5th centile	102/323 (31.6)	57/355 (16.1)	2.41 (1.67–3.49) <0.001
[Data missing]	43	40	

[a] The percentage was calculated from the number of babies for which the information was provided.

Deficiencies in interpretation of tests occurred in 14% of babies who died and in 9% of babies who survived. This difference was just significant, but when the comparison was adjusted for clinical suspicion evidence of being less than the 5th centile it was not (Table 3.3).

Inappropriate actions were identified in 25% of babies who died and in 14% of babies who survived. This difference was significant (Table 3.3).

The staff were not of the appropriate seniority for 12% of mothers of babies who died and 10% of mothers of babies who survived. This difference was not significant (Table 3.3).

Table 3.3 Panel opinion: antepartum assessment of fetal well-being

	Babies who died (%) [a] n = 366	Babies who survived(%) [a] n = 395	Crude OR (95% CI) p value	Adjusted OR [b] (95% CI) p value
Inadequate assessment	91(25.6)	69(17.8)	1.59 (1.12–2.26) 0.01	1.52 (1.03–2.24) 0.04
[Data missing]	11	8		
Inadequate interpretation	48 (14.1)	35 (9.3)	1.59 (1.00–2.53) 0.05	1.42 (0.85–2.38) 0.18
[Data missing]	25	20		
Inappropriate action	86 (24.8)	55 (14.4)	1.95 (1.34–2.84) <0.001	1.61 (1.08–2.42) 0.02
[Data missing]	19	14		
Deficiencies in seniority of staff	36 (11.5)	35 (10.3)	1.12 (0.69–1.84) 0.64	0.92 (0.53–1.61) 0.77
[Data missing]	52	56		

[a] The percentage was calculated from the number of babies for which the information was provided.
[b] Adjusted for predelivery evidence of <5th centile.

ANALYSIS OF COMMENTS

Assessment of fetal well-being

The panels made 181 comments on deficiencies in assessment of fetal well-being: 104 comments related to 91 (25.6%) babies who died and 77 comments related to 69 (17.8%) babies who survived. These are categorised in Table 4.

Deficient investigation usually referred to one or more types of test used to assess fetal well-being. The most frequent comment related to failures to perform umbilical artery Doppler assessment. Problems with ultrasound were divided into failure to perform and poor-quality procedures. At times these failures were due to lack of access to specialist services, either because of the timing of admission or the facilities available at the hospital in which the mother was managed. Comments on CTG reflected the difficulties of interpretation at this gestation and were often related to traces that were too brief to be adequately interpreted.

Suboptimal conduct of fetal well-being tests included poor application of scans with failures to determine chorionicity; to measure liquor volume; to undertake anomaly scans when indicated; and to chart growth measurements. There were also concerns regarding the use of CTGs; these included recordings that were of poor quality and too brief.

Table 3.4 Assessment of fetal well-being: number of comments and percentage of babies involved

	Babies who died n = 366		Babies who survived n = 395	
	Number of comments	Number and (%) [a] of babies n = 355	Number of comments	Number and (%) [a] of babies n = 387
Deficient investigation	38	38 (10.7)	32	32 (8.3)
Doppler	19		13	
Ultrasound	13		13	
CTG	9		7	
Biophysical	8		6	
Other	3		0	
Suboptimal conduct of fetal well-being test	23	23 (6.5)	14	14 (3.6)
Suboptimal follow-on assessment	25	25 (7.0)	11	11 (2.8)
Miscellaneous	18	18 (5.1)	20	20 (5.2)
Comment not given		1		0
Any failure	104	91 (25.6)	77	69 (17.8)

[a] The percentage was calculated from the number of babies for which the information was provided.

Interpretation of fetal well-being tests

The panels made 78 comments on deficiencies in interpretation of the assessments of fetal well-being: 49 comments related to 48 (14.1%) babies who died and 32 comments to 35 (9.3%) babies who survived. These are categorised in Table 3.5.

Table 3.5   Interpretation of fetal well-being tests: number of comments and percentage of babies involved

	Babies who died n = 366		Babies who survived n = 395	
	Number of comments	Number and (%)[a] of babies n = 341	Number of comments	Number and (%)[a] of babies n = 375
Poor interpretation of :				
Ultrasound scan	17	17 (5.0)	13	13 (3.5)
CTG	18	18 (5.3)	11	11 (2.9)
Failure to recognise abnormality	12		4	
Inappropriate interpretation	6		4	
General issue	0		3	
Clinical findings	2	2 (0.6)	2	2 (0.5)
Miscellaneous	9	9 (2.6)	6	6 (1.6)
Comment not given		3		3
Any failure	46	48 (14.1)	32	35 (9.3)

[a]   The percentage was calculated from the number of babies for which the information was provided.

Actions taken

The panels made 141 comments on deficiencies in the actions taken in response to fetal well-being assessments: 88 comments related to 86 (24.8%) babies who died and 53 comments to 55 (14.4%) babies who survived. These are categorised in Table 3.6.

Table 3.6 Actions taken in response to fetal assessment: number of comments and percentage of babies involved

	Babies who died n = 366		Babies who survived n = 395	
	Number of comments	Number and (%)[a] of babies n = 347	Number of comments	Number and (%)[a] of babies n = 381
Inadequate follow-on assessment	19	19 (5.5)	13	13 (3.4)
Inappropriate decision to deliver	19	19 (5.5)	7	7 (1.8)
Failure to act on high-risk situation	14	14 (4.0)	10	10 (2.6)
Delivery should have occurred earlier	11	11 (3.2)	12	12 (3.1)
Failure to complete course of antenatal steroids	4	4 (1.2)	2	2 (0.5)
Inappropriate mode of delivery	4	4 (1.2)	2	2 (0.5)
Poor communication with parents	4	4 (1.2)	0	0
Miscellaneous	13	13 (3.8)	7	7 (1.8)
Comment not given		0		2
Any failure	88	86 (24.8)	53	55 (14.4)

[a]   The percentage was calculated from the number of babies for which the information was provided.

Seniority of staff

The panels made 71 comments on deficiencies in involvement of senior staff: 37 comments related to 36 (11.5%) babies who died and 34 comments to 35 (10.3%) babies who survived. These are categorised in Table 3.7. The most frequent concern related to lack of consultant involvement.

DISCUSSION

Deficiencies in all aspects of antenatal management of fetal well-being occurred more frequently in the babies who died. These included tests performed, interpretation and responses to the findings. In addition, antenatal tests of fetal well-being were more often abnormal in babies who died (Table 3.2). This applied to all tests including CTGs, ultrasound scans, Dopplers and biophysical profiles. Babies who died were more likely to have had umbilical artery Doppler ultrasound scans, indicating antenatal awareness of potential compromise (Neilson and Alfirevic, 2002).

Table 3.7 Seniority of staff: number of comments and percentage of babies involved

	Babies who died n = 366		Babies who survived n = 395	
	Number of comments	Number and (%) [a] of babies n = 314	Number of comments	Number and (%) [a] of babies n = 339
Lack of consultant involvement	21	21 (6.7)	17	17 (5.0)
Care given by SHO	6	6 (1.9)	8	8 (2.4)
Midwifery care issue	2	2 (0.6)	1	1 (0.3)
Miscellaneous	8	8 (2.6)	8	8 (2.4)
Comment not given		0		1
Any failure	37	36 (11.5)	34	35 (10.3)

[a] The percentage was calculated from the number of babies for which the information was provided.

A main aim of the Enquiry was to quantify the effect of clinical care on the outcome of the baby. Antenatal care comprises screening and responding to abnormalities of tests that may indicate underlying pathology. However, a pregnancy with pre-existing pathology will be the target of more complex surveillance and assessment. This relationship precludes accurate evaluation of the individual contributions of pathology and care to the outcome of the baby. Regardless of cause or effect, it is of concern that failures both to assess and to act appropriately occurred in at least 1 in 4 of the babies who died (Table 3.3).

It was not the aim of the Enquiry to address the role of specific antenatal tests, and no specific standards had been provided to panels. However, the most frequent comments related to the lack of umbilical artery Doppler ultrasound scans followed by lack of ultrasound assessment of fetal growth and amniotic fluid (Table 3.4). At times this was thought to be due to a lack of awareness of their value. The use of umbilical Doppler ultrasound is indicated in pregnancies complicated by hypertension and presumed impaired fetal growth (Neilson and Alfirevic, 2002), but its role in other high-risk circumstances is less well defined. This emphasises the need for national guidance on defining the role of Doppler ultrasound in the management of the preterm baby. Tests that might have a positive impact on outcome should be performed if there is a possibility of fetal risk (SOGC Clinical Practice Guidelines). Failures to investigate may at times have been due to difficulties in accessing services such as detailed ultrasound and Dopplers. Ensuring timely and effective access to fetal welfare services is a challenging but extremely important issue for maternity units.

Concerns about the manner in which fetal tests were performed, together with the timing of follow-up assessment (mainly ultrasound scans) were more frequent for babies who died. Clinicians who review fetal tests are required to make plans for either no further action, additional tests or delivery, and their decisions are necessarily dependent on the information they are given. It is therefore essential that all tests are performed correctly by appropriately trained personnel and reported clearly. A plan for further assessment should be made and clearly documented by the reviewing clinician.

An inappropriate decision to deliver was noted three times more frequently in the babies who died than in those who survived (Table 3.6). Although survival of babies at this gestation is now nearly 90% (CESDI 8th Annual Report, 2001), there is still a significant risk of mortality and morbidity, and a decision for delivery should be made only after careful review by an experienced and senior obstetrician.

The seniority of staff was considered appropriate in 90% of circumstances, although the commonest issue regarding staffing was a lack of consultant involvement (Table 3.7); this was equally noted in the mothers of babies who died and in mothers of babies who survived. The concerns about poor responses to investigations and poor decision-making suggest that the management of high-risk pregnancies is a priority area for continuing professional development for all grades of staff.

CONCLUSIONS

Deficiencies in fetal well-being assessments were more frequent in babies who died (26%) than in babies who survived (18%), and this difference was significant. Separating out the effects of underlying pathology of the pregnancy from that of clinical care was problematic. Regardless of cause or effect, there is substantial scope for improvement in assessment of fetal well-being for an anticipated preterm delivery. The role of specific technologies, in particular umbilical artery Doppler ultrasound, need better definition.

RECOMMENDATIONS

At national and commissioning level

3.1 Guidelines should be developed for fetal well-being assessment at 27–28 weeks gestation in women at risk of elective delivery. These should specify the indications for referral for specialist feto-maternal assessment.

At Trust level

Training

3.2 All obstetricians and midwives should receive training and be aware of the indications for fetal well-being tests. These should include preterm CTG, ultrasound and umbilical artery Doppler ultrasound scans. Staff caring for high-risk women should receive training in the interpretation of such tests.

Clinical practice

3.3 Any planned delivery earlier than 27–28 weeks requires review, as early as possible, by staff with appropriate expertise in the interpretation of fetal well-being tests. Women in this group should be seen within 24 hours of admission by a consultant obstetrician and their plan of care reviewed.

Local guidelines

3.4 Units should ensure there are guidelines concerning the assessment of fetal well-being in suspected growth restriction and pre-eclampsia. These should include route of referral, investigations, timescale and follow-up.

Documentation and audit

3.5 There should be local standards, which are regularly reviewed, for the antenatal assessment of fetal well-being.

4 *Antenatal management of preterm delivery*

Preterm delivery is a major cause of perinatal mortality and morbidity. The most effective antenatal intervention is the administration of corticosteroids to the mother: this reduces by a third the risk of both respiratory distress syndrome and neonatal mortality. (Crowley, 2002). This formed the basis of the only prespecified standard within the enquiries relating to the obstetric management of prematurity. Evidence for the value of treatment of chorioamnionitis and the use of tocolysis is less strong, and no specific standards were provided to the panels. This chapter describes these three aspects of the antenatal management of preterm labour: prophylactic corticosteroids, chorioamnionitis and the use of tocolysis. The panels were also given an opportunity to identify other aspects of concern that occurred in the antenatal period, and these are also summarised.

ADMINISTRATION OF CORTICOSTEROIDS

Administration of corticosteroids is not always possible in the event of a rapid unexpected delivery. The panels were asked to identify if there was an opportunity to give corticosteroids, and this was less likely to occur in mothers of babies who died (68%) than in mothers of babies who survived (75%) (Table 4.1).

The optimal interval between treatment and delivery is more than 24 hours but less than 7 days (Crowley, 1998; RCOG 1999). This was achieved in 49% of mothers of babies who died and in 56% of mothers of babies who survived. This difference was statistically significant (Table 4.1). However, when allowance was made for opportunities to administer corticosteroids, the difference became non-significant (Table 4.1).

Repeated courses of corticosteroids were given to 18% of mothers of both groups (Table 4.1).

Table 4.1 Administration of corticosteroids

	Mothers of babies who died (%) [a] n = 352	Mothers of babies who survived(%) [a] n = 371	Crude OR (95% CI) p value	Adjusted [b] OR (95% CI) p value
Opportunity to give a complete course	238 (68.0)	276 (74.6)	0.72 (0.52–1.00) 0.05	
[Data missing]	2	1		
Complete course given >24 h and <7 days before delivery	157 (48.5)	200 (55.9)	0.74 (0.55–1.00) 0.05	0.80 (0.54–1.18) 0.8
[Data missing]	28	13		
>1 course given	60 (17.5)	65 (18.2)	0.96 (0.65–1.41) 0.82	
[Data missing]	9	13		

[a] The percentage was calculated from the number of mothers for which the information was provided.
[b] Adjusted for opportunity to administer corticosteroids.

> **STANDARD: EFFORTS TO ADMINISTER CORTICOSTEROIDS**
>
> Every effort should be made to treat women with a course of corticosteroids prior to preterm delivery. (A course consists of betamethasone 24 mg or dexamethasone 24 mg in divided doses) (Crowley, 1998; RCOG, 1999).

The standard related to the efforts made to administer corticosteroids rather than whether they had been administered or not. The standard was not met in 16% (50/320) of mothers of babies who died and in 11% (37/345) of mothers of babies who survived (Table 4.2). This difference just failed to be significant.

Table 4.2 Standard: efforts to administer corticosteroids

	Mothers of babies who died (%) [a] n = 352	Mothers of babies who survived(%) [a] n = 371	Crude OR (95% CI) p value	Adjusted [b] OR (95% CI) p value
Poor effort to administer corticosteroids	50 (15.6)	37 (10.7)	1.54 (0.98–2.43) 0.06	1.53 (0.96–2.45) 0.07
[Data missing]	32	26		

[a] The percentage was calculated from the number of mothers for which the information was provided.
[b] Adjusted for preterm labour and PROM.

The panels made 87 comments on these deficiencies in corticosteroid administration: 50 comments related to the mothers of babies who died and 37 to the mothers of babies who survived. These are categorised in Table 4.3. Failures to appreciate that corticosteroids were indicated was the most frequent reason identified, followed by delays in administration.

Table 4.3 Efforts to administer corticosteroids: number of comments and percentage of maternities involved

	Mothers of babies who died n = 352		Mothers of babies who survived n = 371	
	Number of comments	Number and (%) [a] of mothers n = 320	Number of comments	Number and (%) [a] of mothers n = 345
Failure to appreciate that corticosteroids were indicated	21	21 (6.6)	9	9 (2.6)
Poor timing of corticosteroids in relation to delivery	18	18 (5.6)	21	21 (6.1)
Corticosteroids should have been given earlier	10		14	
Repeat course should have been given	5		2	
Delivery expedited unnecessarily/ effort not made to delay delivery	3		5	
No opportunity to give corticosteroids	3	3 (1.0)	1	1 (0.3)
Documentation	8	8 (2.5)	5	5 (1.5)
Miscellaneous	0	0	1	1 (0.3)
Any failure	50	50 (15.6)	37	37 (10.7)

[a] The percentage was calculated from the number of mothers for which information was provided.

Discussion

It is well established that the administration of corticosteroids more than 24 hours but less than 7 days before delivery reduces the incidence of respiratory distress syndrome and neonatal mortality (Crowley, 2002). In the present study mothers of babies who died were less likely to receive treatment within this optimal time period. This difference was primarily due to the fewer opportunities for administration in the mothers of babies who died (Table 4.1).

The panels assessed the efforts made by the health professionals to administer steroids, rather than whether they were administered or not. This was considered suboptimal more frequently in cases where the baby died (16%) than in those where the baby survived (11%); this difference only just failed to be statistically significant and suggested a shortfall in care.

The single most common reason for poor attention to corticosteroid management in the maternities where the baby died was a failure to appreciate that corticosteroids were indicated. Health professionals need to be aware of the importance of making every effort to give women prophylactic corticosteroids if there are any clinical features indicating a possible preterm delivery, whether spontaneous or planned.

Delay in administering steroids was the second most frequent problem. There were a variety of reasons: delays in referrals between health professionals, notably the general practitioner and the Accident and Emergency department; and failures of obstetric teams to commence steroids following admission. Prompt referral to the obstetric team is essential, and any delays in administering steroids should be minimised. As it is likely that there is some benefit even when corticosteroids are given less than 24 hours before delivery, every effort should be made to administer them despite the possibility of imminent delivery (Crowley, 2002).

There were circumstances in which steroids were erroneously withheld because of the putative effect on the mother's condition. These included diabetes, chest infection, chorioamnionitis and prednisolone use. None of these situations is a contraindication. Prednisolone does not cross the placenta, unlike betamethasone or dexamethasone.

There should also be clear documentation of when corticosteroids are given. At 27–28 weeks gestation, in-utero transfers occur in 26% of mothers (see Chapter 13) and health professionals at different sites need to have ready access to this information.

There is ambiguity regarding the timing and need for repeat prophylactic courses of antenatal steroids. This was apparent from the panel comments. Steroids should ideally be administered within 1 week of delivery, but this is not always feasible as it is not possible to predict accurately whether or when preterm delivery will occur, and nearly a fifth of these babies had received more than one course of corticosteroids (Table 4.1). Recent concerns have been expressed regarding harmful effects of repeat courses of prophylactic steroids and this topic has been reviewed (Aghajafari et al., 2001). It remains uncertain whether the benefits outweigh the harm: guidelines on timing, dosage and indications need to be regularly reviewed in the light of new findings.

MANAGEMENT OF CHORIOAMNIONITIS

Twenty-five percent of mothers of babies who died and 31% of mothers of babies who survived were managed for *presumed* chorioamnionitis before delivery. *Clinical* chorioamnionitis, defined by the presence of at least one clinical feature, was noted in 10% of mothers of babies who died and in 13% of the mothers of babies who survived (Table 4.4).

Specimens for culture were sent from 51% of mothers of babies who died and from 61% of mothers of babies who survived. Antibiotics were administered to 29% of mothers of babies who died and to 36% of mothers of babies who survived (Table 4.4). These differences were significant, but may have reflected the greater proportion with predelivery evidence of chorioamnionitis in the latter group (Table 4.4).

The specimens comprised: high vaginal swab 87%; blood cultures 15%; endocervical swab 8%; amniotic fluid 1.5%; and others 26%.

Table 4.4 Chorioamnionitis: management; clinical evidence; microbiology; and administration of antibiotics

	Mothers of babies who died (%) [a] n = 352	Mothers of babies who survived(%) [a] n = 371	Crude OR (95% C I) p value	Adjusted [b] OR (95% C I) p value
Managed for presumed chorioamnionitis	84 (24.8)	112 (30.8)	0.74 (0.53–1.03) 0.08	0.69 (0.48–0.99) 0.05
[Data missing]	13	7		
Clinical chorioamnionitis	36 (10.3)	49 (13.2)	0.75 (0.47–1.19) 0.22	0.69 (0.41–1.16) 0.16
[Data missing]	2	1		
Microbiological specimens sent	173 (51.0)	222 (61.2)	0.66 (0.49–0.89) 0.01	0.62 (0.43–0.89) 0.01
[Data missing]	13	8		
Antibiotics administered	99 (29.4)	130 (36.3)	0.73 (0.53–1.00) 0.05	0.67 (0.46–0.98) 0.04
[Data missing]	15	13		

[a] The percentage was calculated from the number of mothers for which information was provided.
[b] Adjusted for preterm labour and PROM.

Panel opinion

In those managed for presumed chorioamnionitis, 19% (16/84) of mothers of babies who died and 23% (26/112) of mothers of babies who survived had deficient or inappropriate care. There was no difference between the mothers of babies who died and mothers of babies who survived (Table 4.5).

Table 4.5 Panel opinion: management of 196 mothers with presumed chorioamnionitis

	Mothers of babies who died (%) n = 84	Mothers of babies who survived(%) n = 112	Crude OR (95% CI) p value	Adjusted[a] OR (95% CI) p value
Deficient or inappropriate care	16 (19.0)	26 (23.2)	0.78 (0.39–1.57) 0.48	0.81 (0.39–1.65) 0.56

[a]   Adjusted for preterm labour and PROM.

The panels made 41 comments on these failures: 16 related to the mothers of babies who died and 26 to mothers of babies who survived. These are categorised in Table 4.6.

Table 4.6 Management of chorioamnionitis: number of comments and percentage of maternities involved

	Mothers of babies who died		Mothers of babies who survived	
	Number of comments	Number and (%)[a] of mothers n = 84	Number of comments	Number and (%)[a] of mothers n = 112
Antibiotic treatment issues	6	6 (7.1)	16	16 (14.3)
Antibiotics delayed or not given	6		11	
Inappropriate use of antibiotics	0		5	
Poor assessment	4	4 (4.8)	6	6 (5.4)
Suboptimal investigation	3		3	
Chorioamnionitis not recognised	0		2	
Diagnosis questionable	1		1	
General management	5	5 (6.0)	4	4 (3.6)
Comment not given		3		1
Any failure	15	16 (19.0)	26	26 (23.2)

[a]   The percentage was calculated from the mothers with presumed chorioamnionitis.

Discussion

Over a quarter of mothers were managed for presumed chorioamnionitis, and in a fifth of these the management was considered to be poor. However, there was no association between concerns about management and the outcome for the baby (death/survival) (Table 4.6).

The commonest concern related to antibiotics being withheld or delayed despite evidence of possible chorioamnionitis. Although routine antibiotics are not recommended for women in preterm labour with intact membranes (SOGC, 2002; Kenyon et al., 2002), evidence of possible intrauterine infection should not be ignored.

USE OF TOCOLYTICS

Tocolysis may be indicated to delay preterm labour in specific circumstances; for example, to enable the transfer of the mother to a unit with appropriate neonatal facilities. However, it is not appropriate in the management of all cases of premature labour. In established labour tocolytics were used in 30% of mothers of babies who died and in 40% of mothers of babies who survived. This difference was statistically significant but may be influenced by the frequency of opportunities to use tocolytics (Table 4.7).

Table 4.7 Tocolytics in established labour (384 mothers)

	Mothers of babies who died (%) n = 173	Mothers of babies who survived(%) n = 211	Crude OR (95% CI) p value	Adjusted[a] OR (95% CI) p value
Use of tocolytics	51 (29.5)	86 (40.8)	0.61 (0.40–0.93) 0.02	0.63 (0.41–0.98) 0.04

[a]   Adjusted for PROM.

Panel opinion

In mothers in established labour, inappropriate use or non-use of tocolytics was noted in 14% (23/169) of the mothers of babies who died and in 17% (35/204) of mothers of babies who survived (Table 4.8). This difference was not statistically significant.

Table 4.8   Panel opinion: tocolytics in established labour (384 mothers)

	Mothers of babies who died (%)[a] n = 173	Mothers of babies who survived(%)[a] n = 211	Crude OR (95% CI) p value	Adjusted[b] OR (95% CI) p value
Inappropriate use or non-use of tocolytics	23 (13.6)	35 (17.2)	0.76 (0.43–1.35) 0.35	0.79 (0.44–1.42) 0.44
[Data missing]	4	7		

[a]   The percentage was calculated from the number of mothers for which information was provided.
[b]   Adjusted for PROM.

The panels made 57 comments on these deficiencies: 23 related to mothers whose babies died and 34 to mothers whose babies survived. These are categorised in Table 4.9. The concerns were similar for both groups of mothers, and issues were divided equally into failures to use tocolytics and inappropriate application.

Table 4.9 Tocolytics in established labour: number of comments and percentage of maternities involved

	Mothers of babies who died n = 173		Mothers of babies who survived n = 211	
	Number of comments	Number and (%)[a] of mothers n = 169	Number of comments	Number and (%)[a] of mothers n = 204
Inappropriate use	8	8 (4.7)	18	18 (8.8)
Labour too far advanced	2		5	
Presence of chorioamnionitis	1		2	
Presence of antepartum haemorrhage	0		4	
Medical condition contraindication	0		3	
Completed full course of corticosteroids	0		2	
Wrong choice of tocolytic	4		0	
General	1		2	
Failures to use	12	12 (7.1)	13	13 (6.4)
General management	7		11	
Delay in diagnosis of preterm labour	4		0	
Discontinued too soon	0		1	
Maternal request	1		1	
Miscellaneous	3	3 (1.8)	3	3 (1.5)
Comment not given		0		1
Any failure	23	23 (13.6)	34	35 (17.2)

[a] The percentage was calculated from the number of mothers for which the information was available.

Discussion

Tocolytics are not indicated in all preterm labours but are relevant in specific circumstances, in particular to allow administration of a complete course of antenatal corticosteroids or to enable transfer of the mother and baby to a unit with appropriate neonatal facilities (RCOG, 1997). They are not indicated in clinical situations where they may be harmful to the mother or fetus.

In the present study tocolytics were less likely to be used in circumstances in which the baby died, and this may have been because of fewer indications. There is no clear evidence that their use improves outcome (RCOG, 1997). Concerns regarding their use or non-use occurred equally in the mothers of babies who died and mothers of babies who survived.

The most frequent issue was inappropriate use in the maternities in which the baby survived. The commonest concern relating to failures to use was that tocolysis might have enabled a complete course of corticosteroids. The choice of tocolytic was not a major issue, although some concerns were expressed regarding the use of products such as indomethacin and glyceryl trinitrate which have not been evaluated adequately. Since the time of the Enquiry, nifedipine and atosiban have also emerged as effective agents with fewer side effects than the more commonly used ritodrine (Clinical Guideline No 1B, RCOG, 2002).

OTHER ASPECTS OF OBSTETRIC CARE

The panels made 207 comments relating to other aspects of obstetric care, and these are categorised in Table 4.10.

Table 4.10   Other aspects of obstetric care: number of comments and percentage of maternities involved

	Mothers of babies who died n = 352		Mothers of babies who survived n = 371	
	Number of comments	Number and (%)^a of mothers n = 348	Number of comments	Number and (%)^a of mothers n = 362
Antenatal management of mother	90	90 (25.9)	79	79 (21.8)
General management issues	43		43	
Antenatal risk assessment	31		18	
No antenatal plan of care	15		14	
Drug issues	1		4	
Maternal lifestyle/relationship	4	4 (1.1)	10	10 (2.8)
Inappropriate vaginal examinations	3	3 (0.9)	5	5 (1.4)
Dating of pregnancy	1	1 (0.3)	3	3 (0.8)
Miscellaneous	8	8 (2.3)	4	4 (1.1)
Any failure	106	106 (30.5)	101	101 (27.9)

^{a} The percentage was calculated from the number of mothers for which information was provided.

This section of the enquiry emphasized panels' concern about antenatal management of the mother rather than the baby. Poor general management and risk assessment were highlighted in a fifth of mothers. This echoes the findings of the panel enquiries into 422 stillbirths occurring in 1996–1997 (CESDI 8th Annual Report, 2001). The need for national evidence-based guidelines on maternal antenatal assessment is reiterated and, although an Antenatal Care Guideline is due in 2003, this does not cover the high-risk mother. Local continuing professional development for health professionals to include this aspect of care is urgently needed.

Inappropriate vaginal examination, including digital vaginal examination in the presence of preterm prelabour rupture of the membranes (PROM), was noted on occasions. Digital vaginal examination may theoretically increase the risk of ascending infection and has been found to shorten the PROM–delivery interval (Lewis, 1992). At the time of first presentation, only a sterile speculum examination should be performed, to confirm the diagnosis and obtain microbiological specimens. Following this, digital vaginal examination should be avoided without a clear indication such as probable spontaneous labour or to exclude cord prolapse.

Infrequently the mother's relationship with the health professional jeopardised optimal maternity care. In some cases there are underlying social issues which require long-term help before they can be resolved, but in many cases resistance to medical help is due to the woman or her partner feeling coerced into decisions that will affect their lives (Egan, 2002). Good communication skills are essential to overcome this so that parents are well-informed and feel a part of the decision-making process. Health professionals should ensure that there is clear documentation of any problems encountered during a woman's management.

CONCLUSION

Mothers of babies who died were less likely to receive corticosteroids, and efforts to ensure that they were administered were considered inadequate in at least 16% of maternities. Further improvements in practice are needed, particularly in the recognition of circumstances in which corticosteroids are indicated.

Clinical chorioamnionitis was not associated with the death of the baby. Inappropriate care of this condition was noted equally in mothers of babies who survived and those who died. Failures to give or delay in giving antibiotics in cases of presumed chorioamnionitis was the main area of panel concern.

In established labour, tocolytics were used in 30% of mothers of babies who died and in 41% of mothers of babies who survived. However, there was no evidence to suggest that the use of tocolytics improved outcome. Their application was inappropriate in 7% of maternities in established labour, but should have been considered in an equivalent number to enable completion of a course of prophylactic corticosteroids.

Although not necessarily impacting on the outcome of the baby poor general management and risk assessment was highlighted in a fifth of mothers, particularly those with medical complications.

RECOMMENDATIONS

At Trust level

Training

4.1 All health professionals who may come into contact with a woman in threatened premature labour need to be aware of the benefits of antenatal administration of corticosteroids and of the difficulties in the diagnosis of premature labour.

Clinical practice

4.2 Units should ensure there is a system to clearly flag mothers who are at risk of preterm delivery at booking and during antenatal care. These mothers should have an appropriate level of consultant care.

4.3 Prompt referral to an obstetrician with appropriate expertise should be made in all cases of threatened preterm labour to assess the need for a tocolytic and to avoid delay in the administration of corticosteroids.

Local guidelines

4.4 Units should ensure there are clear guidelines concerning:

- Antenatal steroid usage, including dosage, timing and criteria. These should be consistent with the RCOG guideline No 7 (RCOG, 1999) and be updated in line with current evidence.

- The management of mothers identified to be at increased risk for preterm delivery at booking and during antenatal care. These should include mothers with multiple pregnancies.

- The indications and contraindications for tocolytics. These should be consistent with the RCOG guideline No 1B (RCOG, 2002).

- The requirement for digital vaginal examination.

5 *Intrapartum care*

Premature labour and delivery is a high-risk situation for mother and baby. Frequently the labour is unexpected and the timing of delivery cannot be planned. The expertise available at the time may therefore be of paramount importance. For this review, panels were asked a series of questions relating to labour and delivery, together with their assessment of the standard of care given.

LABOUR

Onset of labour

Spontaneous labour occurred in the case of 51% (186/366) of babies who died and 57% (227/395) of babies who survived. This difference was not significant (p = 0.07) (Table 5.1). Nearly all babies whose mothers did not go into spontaneous labour were delivered by caesarean section (Table 5.1). A third of the mothers who went into spontaneous labour had multiple pregnancy (130/390) compared to 15% of the mothers who did not (49/333).

Fetal heart rate monitoring and ultrasound

When the mother was in established labour, continuous electronic fetal monitoring was used for 80% of babies who died and 82% of babies who survived. The type of monitoring used was similar for both groups of babies (Table 5.2).

In babies in whom a vaginal delivery was anticipated an ultrasound scan was used to confirm presentation in 59% (90/159) of babies who died and in 54% (106/222) of babies who survived. This difference was significant (p = 0.04).

Table 5.1 Onset of labour and mode of delivery in babies

	Babies who died (%)[a] n = 366	Babies who survived (%)[a] n = 395	Crude OR (95% CI) p value	Adjusted[b] OR (95% CI) p value
Spontaneous labour	186 (51.4)	227 (57.8)	Reference group	Reference group
Vaginal delivery	106 (29.3)	141 (35.9)		
Caesarean section	76 (21.0)	84 (21.4)		
[Data missing]	4	2		
Not in spontaneous labour	180 (49.6)	168 (42.6)	1.31 (0.98–1.74) 0.07[c]	1.29 (0.96–1.73) 0.09[c]
Vaginal delivery	1 (0.3)	3 (0.8)		
Caesarean section	176 (48.5)	164 (41.6)		
[Data missing]	3	1		

[a] The percentage was calculated from the number of babies for which the information was provided.
[b] Adjusted for PROM.
[c] Spontaneous vs non spontaneous labour.

Table 5.2 Fetal heart rate monitoring in spontaneous labour

	Babies who died (%)[a] n = 186	Babies who survived (%)[a] n = 227	Crude OR (95% CI) p value	Adjusted[b] OR (95% CI) p value
Continuous EFM[c]	125 (79.1)	160 (81.6)	Reference group	Reference group
Combination of intermittent auscultation and continuous EFM	12 (7.6)	20 (10.2)	0.77 (0.36–1.63)	0.72 (0.33–1.55)
Intermittent auscultation	21 (13.3)	16 (8.2)	1.68 (0.84–3.35) 0.24[d]	1.61 (0.79–3.25) 0.26[d]
[Data missing]	28	31		

[a] The percentage was calculated from the number of records for which the information was available.
[b] Adjusted for PROM.
[c] EFM, electronic fetal monitoring.
[d] Trend across type of monitoring.

DELIVERY

Indications for delivery

The indication for delivery in the 333 maternities in which labour did not occur spontaneously is shown in Table 5.3. Presumed fetal compromise was the most frequent indication, and was commoner in the mothers of babies who died.

Table 5.3 Indication for delivery in mothers who did not go into spontaneous labour

	Mothers of babies who died (%)[a] n = 173	Mothers of babies who survived (%)[a] n = 160
Presumed fetal compromise/ IUGR/ abnormal CTG	75 (44.1)	54 (34.8)
Pre-eclampsia/ eclampsia/ HELLP	31 (18.2)	44 (28.3)
Antepartum or intrapartum haemorrhage	25 (14.7)	26 (16.8)
Multiple pregnancy	8 (4.7)	3 (1.9)
Other (maternal)	8 (4.7)	9 (5.8)
Chorioamnionitis	6 (3.5)	12 (7.7)
Maternal medical disease	5 (2.9)	1 (0.7)
Other (fetal)	5 (2.9)	3 (1.9)
Previous poor obstetric outcome	3 (1.8)	0
Cord prolapse	2 (1.2)	2 (1.3)
Breech presentation	2 (1.2)	1 (0.7)
[Data missing]	3	5

[a] The percentage was calculated from the number of mothers for which the information was provided.

CTG, cardiotocography; HELLP, haemolysis, elevated liver enzymes, low platelets syndrome; IUGR, intrauterine growth restriction.

Mode of delivery

Most babies were delivered by caesarean section (70% of babies who died and 63% of babies who survived). A higher risk of death was associated with caesarean delivery, but allowing for interval between prelabour rupture of membranes (PROM) and delivery this risk was no longer apparent (Table 5.4). Most caesarean deliveries were carried out through the lower uterine segment, but for 11% of babies who died and 6% of babies who survived the delivery involved the upper uterine segment (Table 5.4).

Table 5.4 Mode of delivery

	Babies who died (%)[a] n = 366	Babies who survived (%)[a] n = 395	Crude OR (95% CI) p value	Adjusted[b] OR (95% CI) p value
Vaginal	107 (29.2)	144 (36.5)	Reference group	Reference group
Spontaneous vaginal cephalic	61 (16.7)	108 (27.3)		
Vaginal breech	40 (10.9)	33 (8.4)		
Forceps	6 (1.6)	3 (0.8)		
Caesarean section	252 (70.2)	248 (63.3)	1.37 (1.01–1.86)	1.10 (0.74–1.61)
Lower segment	214 (59.6)	225 (57.4)	0.04[c]	0.64[c]
Upper segment	38 (10.6)	23 (5.9)		
[Data missing]	7	3		

[a] The percentage was calculated from the number of babies for which the information was provided.

[b] Adjusted for preterm labour and PROM.

[c] Vaginal delivery vs caesarean section.

Caesarean section – degree of urgency

Caesarean section was classified according to the degree of urgency:

- semi-elective or planned emergency – a clinical situation in which delivery is undertaken within 4–12 hours of the decision to deliver
- unplanned emergency – a clinical situation in which delivery is considered necessary within less than 4 hours
- immediate – a clinical situation of impending fetal death, requiring delivery as soon as possible, certainly within 30 minutes.

A third of the caesarean sections were semi-elective or planned procedures (33% of babies who died and 34% of babies who survived) (Table 5.5). The caesarean sections requiring to be done immediately were associated with an increased risk of death and this risk remained after adjustment for PROM and premature labour (Table 5.5).

Table 5.5 Caesarean section: degree of urgency

	Babies who died (%) [a] n = 252	Babies who survived (%) [a] n = 248	Crude OR (95% CI) p value	Adjusted [b] OR (95% CI) p value
Semi-elective/planned emergency	84 (33.3)	83 (33.5)	Reference group	Reference group
Unplanned emergency	86 (34.1)	115 (46.4)		
Immediate	82 (32.5)	50 (20.2)	1.91 (1.27–2.80) 0.002 [c]	2.04 (1.34–3.11) 0.001 [c]

[a] The percentage was calculated from the number of babies for which the information was provided.

[b] Adjusted for preterm labour and PROM.

[c] Semi-elective or unplanned vs immediate caesarean section.

Difficulty in conduct of delivery

Difficulty in the conduct of the delivery was identified for 15% of the babies who died and 10% of the babies who survived. This difference was significant and was due to difficulties at caesarean section rather than at vaginal delivery (Table 5.6).

Interpretation of surveillance

The panels made 101 comments on problems with interpretation: 50 related to 50 (15%) mothers of babies who died and 51 related to 51 (14%) mothers of babies who survived. These are categorised in Table 5.12.

Table 5.12 Interpretation of surveillance during labour: number of comments and percentage of maternities involved

	Mothers of babies who died n = 352		Mothers of babies who survived n = 371	
	Number of comments	Number and (%)[a] of mothers n = 334	Number of comments	Number and (%)[a] of mothers n = 353
Poor interpretation of cardiotocograph	17	17 (5.1)	15	15 (4.3)
Failure to recognise a potential high-risk situation	5	5 (1.5)	10	10 (2.8)
Failure to interpret signs of labour	7	7 (2.1)	8	8 (2.3)
Failure to interpret USS correctly	2	2 (0.6)	0	0
Miscellaneous	13	13 (3.9)	14	14 (4.0)
Comments not related to interpretation of surveillance	6	6 (1.8)	4	4 (1.1)
Any failure	50	50 (15.0)	51	51 (14.4)

[a] The percentage was calculated from the number of mothers for which information was provided.

Actions taken

The panels made 161 comments on inappropriate actions: 81 related to 76 (22%) mothers of babies who died and 80 to 81 (23%) mothers of babies who survived. These are categorised in Table 5.13.

Table 5.13 Actions during labour and delivery: number of comments and percentage of maternities involved

	Mothers of babies who died n = 352		Mothers of babies who survived n = 371	
	Number of comments	Number and (%)[a] of mothers n = 343	Number of comments	Number and (%)[a] of mothers n = 357
Inappropriate clinical decisions made	21	21 (6.1)	20	20 (5.6)
General decisions	12		13	
Inappropriate decision for delivery	9		7	
Delay in delivery	15	15 (4.4)	18	18 (5.0)
Inadequate response to potential high-risk situation	12	12 (3.5)	11	11 (3.1)
Conduct of delivery	11	11 (3.2)	6	6 (1.7)
Monitoring of mother and/or baby	10	10 (2.9)	3	3 (0.8)
Appropriate staff not involved	4	4 (1.2)	15	15 (4.2)
Miscellaneous	8	8 (2.3)	14	14 (3.9)
Any failure	81	76 (22.2)	80	81 (22.7)

[a] The percentage was calculated from the number of mothers for which information was provided.

Seniority of staff

The panels made 86 comments on deficiencies in the seniority of staff: 32 related to 32 (11%) mothers of babies who died and 54 to 53 (17%) mothers of babies who survived. These are categorised in Table 5.14.

Table 5.14 Seniority of staff: number of comments and percentage of maternities involved

	Mothers of babies who died n = 352		Mothers of babies who survived n = 371	
	Number of comments	Number and (%)[a] of mothers n = 297	Number of comments	Number and (%)[a] of mothers n = 310
Lack of consultant obstetrician involvement	23	23 (7.7)	25	25 (8.1)
Lack of registrar involvement	1	1 (0.3)	8	8 (2.6)
Concern re seniority of registrar	1	1 (0.3)	6	6 (1.9)
Lack of medical involvement	1	1 (0.3)	4	4 (1.3)
Midwifery staff	1	1 (0.3)	2	2 (0.7)
Paediatric staff	0	0	1	1 (0.3)
Anaesthetic staff	0	0	1	1 (0.3)
Miscellaneous	5	5 (1.7)	7	7 (2.3)
Any failure	32	32 (10.8)	54	53 (17.1)

[a] The percentage was calculated from the number of mothers for which information was provided.

Analgesia and anaesthesia

Ninety-one per cent (314/345) of mothers of babies who died and 93% (344/368) of mothers of babies who survived had some form of analgesia during labour. For women undergoing caesarean section the most frequent type of anaesthesia was a general anaesthetic (48%, 115/242) for the mothers of babies who died and a spinal anaesthetic (54%, 125/232) in the mothers of babies who survived (Table 5.15).

Table 5.15 Type of analgesia or anaesthesia used during labour and delivery, related to mode of delivery and the outcome of the baby

	Mothers of babies who died (%)[a] n = 352	Mothers of babies who survived (%)[a] n = 371
Vaginal delivery	103 (29.9)	136 (37.0)
General anaesthetic	1	0
Spinal	1	5
Epidural	12	27
Opioids	33	42
Local anaesthetic	8	13
Other	57	57
No analgesia	31	22
Caesarean section	242 (70.1)	232 (63.0)
General anaesthetic	115	94
Spinal	107	125
Epidural	37	34
Opioids	14	19
Local anaesthetic	3	0
Other	6	11
[Data missing]	7	3

[a] The percentage was calculated from the number of mothers for which information was provided.

Inappropriate provision of analgesia or anaesthesia was noted in 10% (34/341) of maternities in which the baby died and in 12% (43/360) of maternities in which the baby survived. This difference was not significant (p = 0.4)

The panels made 80 comments on these deficiencies: 36 related to 34 (10%) mothers of babies who died and 44 to 43 (12%) mothers of babies who survived. These are categorised in Table 5.16.

Table 5.16 Provision of analgesia or anaesthesia: number of comments and percentage of maternities involved

	Mothers of babies who died n = 352		Mothers of babies who survived n = 371	
	Number of comments	Number and (%)[a] of mothers n = 341	Number of comments	Number and (%)[a] of mothers n = 360
Inappropriate type of analgesia/anaesthesia	16	16 (4.7)	28	28 (7.8)
Inappropriate general anaesthetic	7		8	
No or inadequate analgesia	6		4	
Concerns re use of opiates	2		3	
Epidural should have been considered	1		13	
Poor anaesthetic management	9	9 (2.9)	7	7 (1.9)
Inappropriate timing of analgesia	6	6 (1.8)	7	7 (1.9)
Miscellaneous	3	3 (0.9)	2	2 (0.6)
Poor Communication	2	2 (0.6)	0	0
Any failure	36	34 (10.0)	44	43 (11.9)

[a] The percentage was calculated from the number of mothers for which information was provided.

Poor anaesthetic management included: delayed or no anaesthetic involvement in high risk cases; absent or inadequate documentation of assessment and monitoring of the mother, for example, no recording of oxygen saturations during surgery; deficient fluid balance; delays in responding to hypotension and failures to stabilise the mother's condition.

DISCUSSION

All deliveries occurring at 27–28 weeks gestation present a high risk to both mother and baby. Most babies were delivered by caesarean section; most of these procedures were unplanned and many performed as immediate emergencies. These situations require the services of an obstetric team with appropriate expertise and immediate access to theatre facilities. They also demand rapid and effective co-ordination with anaesthetic and neonatal services.

It was reassuring that the panels considered the quality of care in labour to be similar both for the babies who died and for those that survived. However, the Enquiry revealed a number of factors of concern relating to the quality of intrapartum care.

There was an excess of difficult deliveries amongst babies who died in the neonatal period. The commonest difficulty was extracting the baby at the time of caesarean section, frequently occurring when immediate delivery was necessary. A consultant obstetrician was present in nearly half of these circumstances. This compares to an 11% consultant presence at the vaginal delivery of a breech birth where the baby went on to die (1994–1996; CESDI 7th Annual Report, 2000). These figures suggest a considerable improvement in availability of senior obstetric staff. Despite this, just over half of these difficult deliveries were conducted by a specialist registrar. There is a wide variation in seniority and experience within this training grade, and the consultant on call for the labour ward should decide on a case-by-case basis whether it is appropriate for the specialist registrar to operate unsupervised (RCOG/RCM, 1999).

It is also notable that difficult vaginal breech deliveries occurred in more babies who died, usually due to cervical entrapment of the fetal head. However, there is still no randomised control trial evidence for the optimum mode of delivery for these babies (RCOG, 2002).

Senior staff were more likely to be involved and present in the management of labour and delivery in cases in which the baby went on to die. However, in a quarter of maternities the specialist registrar made the decision to deliver the baby or babies and the panels commented on the lack of consultant involvement in the intrapartum care of at least 1 in 12 deliveries (Table 5.14). If possible, consultants should participate in all plans to deliver a preterm infant at this gestation, whether vaginally or by caesarean section.

Concerns about the responses to problems arising during labour were noted in just over a fifth of maternities. Maternity care providers should have easy access to written guidance on the management of high-risk situations. Also, continuing professional development programmes should focus on the development needs of health professionals in order to improve the provision of safe and effective maternity care (RCOG, 2000). Problems arising as a result of simultaneous emergencies are highlighted in Chapter 12.

Nearly a tenth of babies were delivered by upper segment caesarean section, which is likely to impact significantly on future pregnancies in these mothers (Halperin et al., 1988). A lower segment incision is often possible at 27–28 weeks gestation unless there are complicating factors such as fibroids or extreme intrauterine growth restriction, and further study of this particular category of deliveries may be useful to guide future practice.

Spontaneous labour was associated with lower mortality rates, although this was of borderline significance. This may be because the mothers who did not go into labour were more likely to have a serious underlying pathology which prompted delivery. Concerns in surveillance were noted in at least 16% of cases (Tables 5.11 and 5.12). Poor quality fetal heart traces were noted, together with problems in interpretation, although it is acknowledged that interpretation at this gestation is even more fraught with difficulties than in the mature fetus. Awareness of these issues should be included in the training for obstetricians and midwives. Ultrasound was used to confirm the fetal presentation in only half the cases in which vaginal delivery was anticipated. Clinical estimation of fetal presentation at this gestation is not always accurate and ultrasound should be used to confirm the findings wherever practicable.

Failures in the provision of anaesthesia or analgesia occurred in just over 10% of labours. Maternity care involves both the mother and the baby and the health and the care received of both can interact and affect outcome. The anaesthetist is an important and essential part of the multidisciplinary team. General anaesthesia is associated with significant complications (Holdcroft and Thomas, 2000) and should be reserved for situations in which the fetal or maternal condition precludes regional anaesthesia. This group of women is at high risk of urgent Caesarean section and the early involvement of the anaesthetist is crucial as the siting of epidural analgesia for pain relief is advocated (Morgan et al., 1990). In preterm labour this enables a controlled, atraumatic vaginal delivery, is not associated with neonatal drug depression and allows for emergency caesarean section if necessary. Education and training to recognise these indications and adequate service provision to allow anaesthetic time to secure epidural nerve blocks in women with premature babies would reduce inappropriate general anaesthetics.

Fluid balance was an area of concern. In this group of women the combination of corticosteroid administration, use of tocolytics and fluid requirements for regional nerve block can all compound to induce circulatory overload. Accurate fluid balance charts should be maintained. There were also examples of poor monitoring of the mother's condition. There are professional guidelines (Holdcroft, 2000) and these include the recording of oxygen saturation during regional nerve blocks. These risk management issues should be reviewed locally by audit of anaesthetic records.

Only two comments were made on cases in which the language barrier resulted in inadequate provision of analgesia, but the emotional impact this may have had on the mother should not be underestimated. Maternity units should give consideration to the provision of 24-hour interpreting services for the benefit of significant ethnic minority groups within the local population.

CONCLUSIONS

Labour at 27–28 weeks gestation is a high-risk situation. Most mothers will require an emergency caesarean section and in a tenth of these the delivery of the baby is technically difficult.

The Enquiry revealed concerns relating to the quality of intrapartum care in a fifth of pregnancies and unsatisfactory provision of anaesthesia or analgesia in a tenth of cases. Despite this, it was somewhat reassuring that these failures did not appear to be directly associated with the death of the baby.

Consultant staff were more likely to be involved with the management and attend deliveries in which the baby died; they were present at just under half of difficult caesarean deliveries. When compared with earlier surveys, these findings imply an improvement in availability of senior staff for emergency care. However, there is still a shortfall with concerns expressed about lack of consultant involvement in 1 in 12 deliveries.

RECOMMENDATIONS

Terms indicated in **bold** are defined in the Glossary (p. xv).

At national and commissioning level

5.1 The need for high-risk delivery suite teams needs to be defined, including training requirements for obstetricians, anaesthetists and midwives.

5.2 The practice of and associated complications with upper segment caesarean section need to be reviewed because of the increased morbidity in subsequent pregnancies.

At Trust level

Clinical practice

5.3 The labour and delivery of babies born at 28 weeks gestation or less should be managed by a high-risk team. The team should include an experienced obstetrician (Calman 4–5 or consultant), anaesthetist and senior midwife with high-risk training in this field.

5.4 The method and timing of an elective delivery of a baby at 28 weeks gestation or less should always be discussed with a consultant obstetrician together with anaesthetic and paediatric colleagues.

5.5 A decision to undertake emergency caesarean section should be discussed with an experienced obstetrician (Calman 4–5 or consultant).

5.6 A delivery by caesarean section of a baby at 28 weeks gestation or less should be performed or supervised by an experienced obstetrician (Calman 4–5 or consultant).

5.7 The conduct of a vaginal delivery of a baby at 28 weeks gestation or less should be performed or supervised by a member of the high-risk team.

Local guidelines

5.8 Units should ensure there are guidelines concerning the intrapartum care of the mother and her preterm baby. These should include:

- communication with the high-risk team and other professionals
- administration of corticosteroids, including dosage, timing and criteria (see Chapter 4)
- indications and contraindications for tocolytics (see Chapter 4)
- management of suspected chorioamnionitis (see Chapter 4)
- requirement for digital vaginal examinations (see Chapter 4)
- monitoring of the baby during labour
- use of analgesia and anaesthetics
- management of the high-risk mother.

Documentation and audit

5.9 There should be local standards, which are regularly reviewed, for the management of high-risk preterm labour and delivery.

5.10 The indication for an upper segment caesarean section should be clearly documented.

6 *Neonatal resuscitation*

Resuscitation is the process of artificially maintaining the airway, breathing and circulation in a patient when the respiratory or cardiovascular system fails. In the newborn infant the problem is usually respiratory. Most infants born at 27–28 weeks gestation have an immature respiratory system and will require resuscitation by skilled staff.

Panels addressed the quality of resuscitation for babies born at 27–28 weeks gestation from the time of birth to admission to the neonatal unit. The care was assessed using four standards for well-established resuscitation techniques and one standard for minimum staff requirements. These standards have been extensively promoted by the RCPCH and the RCOG (BPA, 1993; RCPCH/RCOG, 1997). The panels were also asked to identify areas of concern relating to resuscitation and the transfer of the baby from the labour ward to the neonatal unit.

CONDITION OF THE BABY FROM BIRTH TO ADMISSION TO THE NEONATAL UNIT

Clinical condition of the babies

Nearly all babies were resuscitated at birth: 97% (355/366) of babies who died and 92% (365/395) of babies who survived. Table 6.1 describes the condition of the baby at birth up to admission to the neonatal unit. The babies who died were in worse condition at the time of birth than the babies who survived. Of the babies who died, 9% had no heart rate and 41% had no respiratory activity at birth. This compares to 1% with no heart rate and 19% with no respiratory activity in babies who survived. By the time of admission to the neonatal unit 21% of the babies who died had ineffective respiratory activity or a persistent slow heart rate, compared to 8% in the group that survived.

Table 6.1 Clinical condition of the babies from birth to admission to the neonatal unit

	Babies who died (%) [a] n = 366	Babies who survived (%) [a] n = 395	Crude OR (95% CI) p value
No heart rate at birth	31/352 (8.8)	4/386 (1.0)	9.22 (3.22–26.4) < 0.001
No spontaneous respiratory activity at birth	139/336 (41.4)	68/368 (18.5)	3.11 (2.21–4.38) < 0.001
Absent or ineffective respiratory activity or persistent heart rate <100 beats/min at 1 min	235/340 (69.1)	160/363 (44.0)	2.84 (2.1–3.88) < 0.001
Absent or ineffective respiratory activity or persistent heart rate <100 beats/min at 5 min	135/331 (40.8)	59/361 (16.3)	3.26 (2.47–5.03) < 0.001
Heart rate <60 beats/min at any stage despite effective IPPV	57/310 (18.4)	14/368 (3.8)	5.7 (3.11–10.45) < 0.001
Absent or ineffective respiratory activity or persistent heart rate <100 beats/min on admission to the neonatal unit	67/320 (20.9)	31/375 (8.3)	2.94 (1.86–4.63) < 0.001

[a] The percentage was calculated from the number of babies for which the information was provided.

Drugs administered at any time during resuscitation

Panels were asked which drugs were administered at any time during resuscitation. These are summarised in Table 6.2.

Table 6.2 Drugs administered during resuscitation

Drugs used during resuscitation	Babies resuscitated who died (%) [a] n = 355	Babies resuscitated who survived (%) [a] n = 365	Crude OR (95% CI) p value
Adrenaline	60 (16.9)	13 (3.6)	5.79 (3.12–10.75) < 0.001
[Data missing]	8	8	
Sodium bicarbonate	34 (9.6)	2 (0.6)	20.1 (4.79–84.24) <0.001
[Data missing]	9	11	
Volume expander	58 (16.4)	14 (3.9)	5.1 (2.79–9.33) <0.001
[Data missing]	7	10	
Glucose	28 (7.9)	8 (2.2)	3.54 (1.64–7.6) 0.001
[Data missing]	11	14	

[a] The percentage was calculated from the number of babies for which the information was provided.

Other drugs cited included surfactant (23 babies at birth during the initial resuscitation), naloxone (7), blood (2) and calcium gluconate (2).

Time of admission to the neonatal unit

The time of admission to the neonatal unit ranged from 2 minutes to 89 minutes after birth. The median time of admission to the neonatal unit was 18 (interquartile range [IQR] 11–30) minutes for the babies who died and 18 (IQR 12–28) minutes for the babies who survived (p = 0.93, Mann–Whitney test). The majority (60%, 386/640) of babies were admitted to the neonatal unit by 20 minutes, but 4% of babies who died and 2% of babies who survived were admitted after 50 minutes of life (Figure 6.1).

Figure 6.1   Time of admission to the neonatal unit

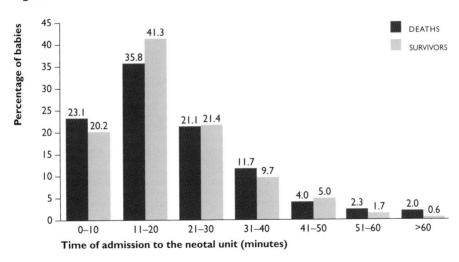

STANDARDS: NEONATAL RESUSCITATION

Five neonatal resuscitation standards were used to assess the care the babies received. One related to the personnel present at delivery; the others related to proficiency in neonatal resuscitation at 1 and 5 minutes after delivery and on admission to the neonatal unit.

STANDARDS FOR NEONATAL RESUSCITATION

a Personnel present for resuscitation: Intermediate grade paediatric staff and/or a consultant neonatal paediatrician, in addition to a junior paediatrician from the neonatal unit, should be present for the delivery (BPA, 1993)

b In the first minute after birth: If there are absent or ineffective respirations or persistent heart rate of <100 beats/minute, then IPPV should be administered via a bag and mask or tracheal intubation without delay (RCPCH/RCOG, 1997)

c 5 minutes after birth: If there is absent or ineffective respiration or a persistent heart rate of <100 beats/minute, then IPPV should be administered via a tracheal tube (Project 27/28 Working Group; CESDI 6th Annual Report, 1999)

d At any time during resuscitation: If at any age the heart rate is <60 beats/minute after effective IPPV has been established, external chest compression should be performed (RCPCH/RCOG, 1997)

e On admission to the neonatal unit: If there is absent or ineffective respiration or a persistent heart rate of <100 beats/minute, then mechanical ventilation should be administered via a tracheal tube (in some cases CPAP may be appropriate) (Project 27/28 Working Group; CESDI 6th Annual Report, 1999)

Standard a: personnel present for resuscitation

The question regarding who was present at delivery was poorly answered, with information available only for 606 babies. For those babies where the information was available a doctor or an advanced neonatal nurse practitioner (ANNP) was present for the majority (95%, 573/606) (Figure 6.2). For half (56%, 338/606) of the deliveries there was a combination of consultant or intermediate grade doctor in addition to a senior house officer (SHO) or ANNP. Consultants were present in 22% (66/298) cases of babies who died and 10% (31/308) of babies who survived. A middle grade without a consultant was present for 60% (180/298) cases of babies who died and 66% (203/308) cases of babies who survived.

Standard a was considered to be achieved if an ANNP or an SHO attended the delivery with a consultant or intermediate grade doctor. Standard a was attained for 54% (162/298) of babies who died and 56% (174/308) of babies who survived (Table 6.3).

Information about who was not present at the time of birth but arrived later for resuscitation was also poorly answered. From the information available, a senior or intermediate grade doctor arrived later for resuscitation for 29% (40/137) of babies who died and 16% (16/102) of survivors.

Figure 6.2 Personnel present for resuscitation ('Intermediate grade doctor' includes specialist registrars and staff grade doctors.)

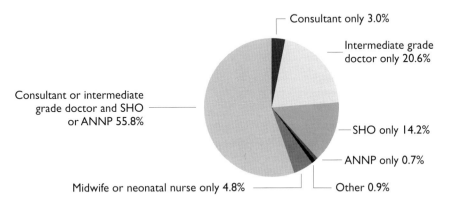

Standards b–e: proficiency in neonatal resuscitation

The four standards relating to proficiency in neonatal resuscitation were more frequently attained (Table 6.3). Standard b was achieved in 97% of the babies who died, standard c in 82%, standard d in 90% and standard e in 91%. Similar levels were observed in the babies who survived (Table 6.3).

Table 6.3 Resuscitation standards

	Standard	Babies who died (%) [a] n = 366	Babies who survived %) [a] n = 395	Crude OR (95% C I) p value	Adjusted [b] OR (95% C I) p value
a	Insufficient staff	136/298 (45.6)	134/308 (43.5)	1.09 (0.79–1.50) 0.60	1.12 (0.81–1.55) 0.50
b	Poor response at minute 1	7/224 (3.1)	7/158(4.4)	0.70 (0.24–2.02) 0.51	0.68 (0.23–1.99) 0.48
c	Poor response at minute 5	24/134 (17.9)	14/59 (23.7)	0.70 (0.33–1.48) 0.35	0.74 (0.35–1.58) 0.44
d	Failures of external chest compression	6/57 (10.5)	3/14 (21.4)	0.43 (0.09–1.99) 0.28	0.44 (0.09–2.04) 0.29
e	Failures to ventilate on admission	6/65 (9.2)	2/31 (6.5)	1.47 (0.28–7.76) 0.65	1.36 (0.26–7.24) 0.72

[a] The percentage was calculated from the number of babies for which the information was provided.
[b] Adjusted for sex and birthweight ≤5th centile.

PANEL OPINION

Panels considered that some aspect of care relating to resuscitation and the initial transfer to the neonatal unit was deficient for 38% (135/360) of babies who died and 24% (95/389) of babies who survived. This difference was statistically significant (Table 6.4).

Table 6.4 Panel opinion: care during resuscitation and transfer to the neonatal unit

Standard	Babies who died (%)[a] n = 366	Babies who survived %)[a] n = 395	Crude OR (95% C I) p value	Adjusted[b] OR (95% C I) p value
Deficiencies in resuscitation	135 (37.5)	95 (24.4)	1.86 (1.36–2.54) <0.001	1.85 (1.34–2.55) <0.001
[Data missing]	6	6		

[a] The percentage was calculated from the number of babies for which the information was provided.
[b] Adjusted for sex and birthweight ≤5th centile.

The panels made 375 comments on these deficiencies: 222 related to the babies who died and 133 to babies who survived. These are categorised in Table 6.5.

DISCUSSION

Nearly all the babies (97%) were resuscitated at birth. This reinforces the importance of provision, attainment and maintenance of skill in resuscitation of preterm babies at this gestation.

Because of the acute nature of resuscitation the standards are based on a consensus of expert opinion rather than on trial evidence. Their assessment was determined from medical records and was therefore not subject to variation in panel opinion. Standards relating to proficiency in neonatal resuscitation were often achieved, whereas the standard relating to staffing levels was achieved in just over half. However, failures to meet the standards did not appear to be associated with an increased risk of death.

Despite the frequent achievement of four of the proficiency standards, the panels had concerns regarding the quality of care in resuscitation and transfer to neonatal unit for 31% of the babies reviewed. These concerns were significantly more frequent in the babies who died (38%) than in the babies who survived (24%), which suggests a relationship between poor care at the time of resuscitation and the risk of death. However, the difference between the two groups may have been overestimated by two factors: the fact that the assessors were aware of the outcome, and the difficulty of managing sicker babies.

Table 6.5   Care during resuscitation and transfer to the neonatal unit: number of comments and percentage of babies involved

	Babies who died (%) n = 366		Babies who survived (%) n = 395	
	Number of comments	Number and (%)[a] of babies n = 360	Number of comments	Number and (%)[a] of babies n = 389
Proficiency in neonatal resuscitation (1, 2 and 3)	112	82 (22.8)	51	48 (12.3)
1 Intubation difficulties	52	49 (13.6)	36	34 (8.7)
Failure to intubate when necessary	18		12	
Multiple intubation attempts	12		7	
Delays in intubating	9		9	
Incorrect size ETT used	6		4	
Misplacement of ETT	3		2	
Inappropriate intubation	2		2	
Miscellaneous	2		0	
2 Other areas relating to proficiency	36	34 (9.4)	5	5 (1.3)
Delayed or no external cardiac massage	8		1	
Thermal care (hypothermia)	7		2	
Incomplete assessment of the baby	6		0	
Resuscitation stopped too soon	5		0	
No cord gases performed	5		0	
Inappropriate procedure performed	3		2	
Resuscitation attempts too aggressive	2		0	
3 Drug errors and equipment failure	24	20 (5.5)	10	10 (2.6)
Failure to treat	7		5	
Wrong dose	9		0	
Equipment failure	4		2	
Unnecessary treatment	3		2	
Incorrect route of drug administration	1		1	
Documentation	45	43 (11.9)	36	35 (9.0)
General comments	22		24	
Lack of details about personnel present	14		7	
Lack of details about treatment	9		5	
Staffing issues	36	29 (8.1)	22	21 (5.4)
Needed consultant /senior involvement	16		6	
SHO unsupported	11		7	
No paediatrician present at delivery	7		9	
No assistance	2		0	
Transfer difficulties	18	18 (5.0)	13	13 (3.3)
Delays in transfer	7		4	
Not stabilised before transfer	8		2	
Inappropriate mode of transfer	2		4	
No monitoring during transfer	1		2	
Inappropriate respiratory support	0		1	
Miscellaneous	11	11 (2.5)	11	11 (2.8)
Any failure	222	135 (37.5)	133	95 (24.4)

[a]   The percentage was calculated from the number of babies for which an opinion was provided.

Most of the concerns raised by the panels described problems with proficiency in neonatal resuscitation. Other notable problems related to staffing, transfer to the neonatal unit and poor documentation.

Proficiency in neonatal resuscitation

Systematic application of resuscitation techniques has become commonplace since the introduction of advanced paediatric life support (APLS) and paediatric advanced life support (PALS) courses in 1992 and more recently neonatal life support (NLS) courses. Although not formally assessed by randomised control trial, these changes, together with national recommendations (BPA, 1993; RCPCH/RCOG, 1997), are likely to have led to widespread achievement of the neonatal resuscitation standards (Patel, 2002) as evidenced by the current Enquiry.

The greater number of failures in standard c (the need to provide IPPV at 5 minutes after birth if there is absent/ineffective respiration or a persistent heart rate of less than 100 beats/minute) and standard d (to apply external chest compression if the heart rate is less than 60 beats/minute) emphasise the need to reinforce these aspects of resuscitation training.

Difficulties and delays with intubation were the most frequent concern raised by the panels. This may explain in part why the standard least likely to be met was the one stating criteria for intubation at 5 minutes after birth. Opportunities to acquire and maintain the ability to intubate a neonate have become less frequent because of an increase in the number of paediatric trainees and also, paradoxically, because of improvements in condition of babies at birth. Ensuring adequate training and competency in this skill is a priority in neonatal care.

Failures and delays in applying external cardiac massage were more frequently commented on in the babies who died. Other problems noted included poor thermal care and assessment of the baby. At times resuscitation was stopped too soon.

A minority of babies required drugs as part of resuscitation. The outcome for these babies was particularly poor. It is notable that more drug errors were reported in babies who died. Infrequent drug use and consequent poor knowledge may lead to errors. Written drug protocols should be readily available on all resuscitaires.

Although equipment failures were rare, checking of equipment is a simple task of paramount importance and should be routine.

Staffing

The only standard that was often not met was standard a, relating to the appropriate staff at delivery. The most frequent concern of the panels, especially for babies who died, was the need for more senior involvement or consultant presence at the time of resuscitation. Neonatal consultant presence of itself is not a requirement, but did occur in 16% of babies. Although it is not routine there are more complex circumstances where senior involvement or support is appropriate. This contrasts with the more frequent involvement of senior obstetric staff at the time of delivery of babies who died (see Chapter 5). Thus either the concern recognised antenatally is not adequately communicated between the obstetric and neonatal teams, or there is a lack of readily available neonatal expertise.

An unsupervised SHO or an ANNP was the most senior person present for 15% of deliveries reviewed. It is of particular concern that 5% of these deliveries were unattended at birth by any paediatric staff. Skilled assistance should be anticipated and sought sooner rather than later. An on-site intermediate grade doctor proficient in advanced resuscitation technique should always be called and be in attendance when the baby is delivered.

Documentation

Thorough documentation of assessments and actions during resuscitation is essential for continuity of clinical care, for communication and to address medicolegal concerns (Kattwinkel et al., 1999). In the present study, two-thirds of medical notes did not provide adequate information about those present at resuscitation. Poor record-keeping weakens the assessment of performance and may help to explain why it appears that the personnel present at delivery failed to meet the expected standard in over half the deliveries.

Transfer between the labour ward and admission to the neonatal unit

Delays and failures to stabilise the baby before transfer were the most frequent issues cited, more so in the babies who died. The median time of admission to the neonatal unit was 18 minutes. However, 7% of babies in the study were admitted to the neonatal unit beyond 50 minutes of age. Such delays should be addressed, although they may be unavoidable due to prolonged resuscitation or excessive distance between labour ward and the neonatal unit. Staff should be experienced in stabilising babies before transfer, and babies should be transferred to the neonatal unit in a transport incubator with appropriate monitoring. In particular, those who have been intubated should be transported to the neonatal unit with continued ventilatory support (BAPM, 1999).

CONCLUSIONS

Although most basic resuscitation requirements for premature babies were achieved, the Enquiry identified a problem relating to the *timely* attendance of *skilled* staff at the delivery of preterm infants in 45% of deliveries. The validity of this concern was impaired by poor documentation of the circumstances surrounding delivery. In future this could be avoided by the provision of a standard reporting form relating to delivery events. Issues with intubation skills were particularly highlighted, and were more frequent in babies who died (14%) than in those babies who survived (9%). Ensuring the availability of skilled personnel is a priority for the well-being of these babies.

RECOMMENDATIONS

Terms indicated in **bold** are defined in the Glossary (p. xv).

At national and commissioning level

6.1 Professional organisations need to agree a specification for a national standard resuscitation record sheet to include personnel present, timing of events and actions taken, as well as equipment issues.

6.2 Commissioners should work with Trusts to introduce common documentation.

At Trust level

Training

6.3 The staff responsible for the immediate care of a baby born at 28 weeks gestation or less should be providers trained in neonatal life support. At least one should be skilled in tracheal intubation.

Clinical practice

6.4 Anticipated deliveries at 28 weeks gestation or less should take place where sufficient trained staff and equipment are present (see Chapter 12).

6.5 All maternity units, of what ever size, must have at least one professional available at all times who is trained in resuscitation and stabilisation of a preterm baby (see Chapter 12).

6.6 Staff responsible for the immediate care of a baby born at 28 weeks gestation or less should be experienced in stabilisation of the baby, with particular reference to airway and temperature control, prior to and during transfer to the neonatal intensive care unit (NICU).

Local guidelines

6.7 Units should ensure that there are guidelines concerning the circumstances in which senior or consultant neonatal staff should attend preterm deliveries.

Documentation and audit

6.8 The time of admission to the neonatal unit following delivery should be monitored and circumstances leading to delay in admission should be reviewed.

died in the first 24 hours were removed from the analysis a low admission temperature was still associated with the death of the baby. Even so, an admission temperature of 36°C is harder to attain in a critically ill baby at birth and this may explain some of the difference that continued to be observed rather than just poor care. Condition of the baby at 5 minutes of age is a marker of illness severity and of the amount of resuscitation required and hence of cold exposure. After adjusting for condition of the baby 5 minutes after birth, there were only minor changes in odds ratios (from 1.91 to 1.71, still significant with $p = 0.002$) of the association between hypothermia on admission to the neonatal unit and death.

As most babies, regardless of outcome, had a temperature of less than 36°C on admission, the feasibility of achieving this standard must be questioned. This chosen value was based on a consensus of expert opinion, indirectly supported by trial evidence that showed reduced mortality when the incubator temperature is adjusted to maintain an anterior abdominal skin temperature above 36°C (Sinclair, 2001). This standard therefore remains an objective of good care. Simple measures such as occlusion wrapping in the delivery room improve early temperature control in babies born at less than 28 weeks gestation (Vohra et al., 1999). Ensuring a correct environmental temperature is also important and the temperature of the delivery room should be at least 25°C (WHO, 1997).

The panels considered that there had been substandard early thermal care in over a third of the babies. This was associated with the babies who died, and remained the case after adjustment for condition of the baby at birth.

Further detail of why the thermal care was substandard was often not given by the panel but corresponded to observations of a 'cold' baby or a temperature of less than 36°C. Specific aspects of substandard care were noted more frequently in the babies who died (17%) than in those who survived (9%). As with the other neonatal assessments, the fact that the assessors were aware of the outcome of the babies may have influenced the more unfavourable comments in the deaths.

Three aspects of substandard care were notably more frequent in the babies who died: allowing the temperature to fall, lack of monitoring and transfer difficulties. Falls in temperature occur during resuscitation and routine procedures (Mok et al., 1991). Incubator temperatures fall when doors are opened. Health professionals working over an infant on a radiant heater may block the heating source (Gunn and Bennet, 2001). Minimal handling will reduce cold stress, and invasive procedures should be carried out in a temperature-controlled environment.

The time taken to normalise the baby's temperature had an unexpectedly large range. Prolonged delay in warming was more frequent than too rapid warming and occurred both in babies who died and in those who survived. Too rapid warming was observed in a few of the babies who died. The optimum warming technique and rate are not established, and there is a need for further research.

Guidance on thermal care is conspicuously absent from the current guidelines for good practice in management of respiratory distress (RCPCH/RCOG, 1997; BAPM, 1999). Guidance in this area is required to ensure awareness of its importance.

CONCLUSIONS

Most babies admitted to the neonatal unit from the labour ward had a temperature below the recommended standard of 36°C. This calls into question the feasibility of achieving the standard. The time taken to normalise the baby's temperature was highly variable, reflecting the fact that the optimum warming technique is not established.

Hypothermia on admission to the neonatal unit and deficiencies in early thermal care were observed more frequently amongst babies who died. Particular areas highlighted included allowing the temperature to fall unnecessarily, lack of monitoring and hypothermia consequent to transfer difficulties.

There is no national guidance on thermal care. Existing policies, practice and equipment should be reviewed. Simple measures to avoid hypothermia should be routine and might significantly improve outcomes of preterm babies.

RECOMMENDATIONS

Terms indicated in **bold** are defined in the Glossary (p. xv).

At Trust level

Training

7.1 All labour ward and paediatric staff should be trained in the thermal care of infants at resuscitation.

Clinical practice

7.2 All transfers of preterm infants from place of delivery to neonatal unit should take place in a warmed transport incubator.

7.3 The temperature of the baby should be recorded and documented within 30 minutes of delivery and thereafter at least at 4-hourly intervals

7.4 Current evidence suggests that efforts should be made to normalise the temperature of hypothermic infants.

7.5 Continuous recording of temperature is necessary for infants requiring intensive care.

Equipment and organisation

7.6 The temperature of the delivery room should normally be at least 25°C (WHO, 1997).

7.7 Incubators should be capable of maintaining appropriate temperature and humidity and should be regularly checked.

PANEL OPINION

Some aspect of surfactant therapy was considered deficient in 32% (113/358) of the babies who died and 21% (81/390) of the babies who survived. This difference was statistically significant (Table 8.5).

Table 8.5 Panel opinion: deficiencies in surfactant therapy

	Babies who died (%)[a] n = 366	Babies who survived (%)[a] n = 395	Crude OR (95% CI) p value	Adjusted[b] OR (95% CI) p value
Deficiencies in surfactant therapy	113 (31.6)	81 (20.8)	1.76 (1.12–2.76) 0.001	1.92 (1.33–2.78) <0.001
[Data missing]	8	5		

[a] The percentage was calculated from the number of babies for which the information was provided.
[b] Adjusted for sex, birthweight ≤5th centile and condition of baby at 5 minutes of age.

The panels made 229 comments on these deficiencies: 134 related to babies who died and 95 to babies who survived. These are categorised in Table 8.6.

Table 8.6 Surfactant therapy: number of comments and percentage of babies involved

	Babies who died n = 366		Babies who survived n = 395	
	Number of comments	Number and (%)[a] of babies n = 358	Number of comments	Number and (%)[a] of babies n = 390
Drug administration problems	101	94 (26.3)	73	65 (16.7)
Delay in administering surfactant	70		52	
Surfactant not administered	9		12	
Inappropriate administration	11		8	
Type of surfactant used queried	5		0	
2nd or 3rd dose of surfactant administered too early	3		1	
Surfactant overdose	2		0	
Surfactant under dose	1		0	
Documentation	22	22 (6.1)	11	11 (2.8)
Intubation difficulties	6	6 (1.7)	5	5 (1.3)
Surfactant not available	2	2 (0.6)	0	0
Miscellaneous	3	3 (0.8)	6	6 (1.5)
Any failure	134	113 (31.6)	95	81 (20.8)

[a] The percentage was calculated from the number of babies for which the information was provided.

DISCUSSION

Surfactant administration to babies who were intubated was nearly universal (96%). This probably reflects clear national recommendations (BAPM, 1999; RCPCH, 2000) that are based on a large body of research evidence (Soll, 1998). However, compliance with the timing of administration (first dose as soon as practical after birth) was much lower (61%) and the concern most frequently expressed by the panels related to these delays.

At the time of the Enquiry synthetic surfactants were still in use in the UK and the type of surfactant used was investigated. Most babies (81%) received natural surfactants. Synthetic surfactants were used significantly more frequently in babies who died (18%) than in those who survived (11%). These Enquiry findings are in keeping with clinical trials and a meta-analysis showing a greater early improvement in ventilatory requirements, fewer air leaks and fewer deaths associated with natural surfactants (Ainsworth et al., 2000; Soll and Blanco, 2001).

Multiple doses of natural surfactant result in better oxygenation and ventilation, fewer air leaks and a trend towards fewer deaths than in cases in which a single dose was used (Soll, 2001). Most babies in the Enquiry (82%) received at least two doses (Figure 8.2).

Two aspects of surfactant administration are unclear: the criteria defining 'at risk' for RDS in babies born at 27–28 weeks and the precise timing for initial administration of surfactant.

In this Enquiry 88% of infants received surfactant; 9% (35/359) of babies who survived did not because they were not thought to be 'at risk' of RDS (Table 8.3). It is unclear as to what criteria determine the infant at risk of RDS, and it remains uncertain how determined physicians should be regarding demonstration of lung immaturity before administration of surfactant. Should all babies receive surfactant prophylactically? A systematic review concluded that prophylactic surfactant compared to selective use reduces the risks of pneumothorax, of pulmonary interstitial emphysema and of mortality in infants at risk of developing RDS (Soll and Morley, 2001). Most studies in the review pertained to all infants born at less than 30 weeks and excluded major congenital anomalies. Some studies also excluded babies with mature lung profiles and those who had prolonged rupture of membranes. Whether this justifies a 'wait and watch' policy at 27–28 weeks is questionable.

The wide distribution of timing of the first dose (Figure 8.1) suggested that a significant proportion of babies did not have prophylactic administration but rather were treated when signs of RDS appeared. Babies who died might show signs of RDS earlier than those who survived. However, surfactant was not given significantly earlier in this group; furthermore, the overriding concern of the panels, more commonly noted in the deaths, was delay in administration of surfactant (Table 8.6).

A precise time for initial administration has not been defined. Treatment is less effective when given later in the course of RDS (OSIRIS Collaborative Group, 1992). Most of the data in the early administration trials pertained to administration within 15 minutes of birth (Egberts et al., 1997; Curley and Halliday, 2001). However, there is evidence that initial stabilisation and immediate postventilatory administration may be a more appropriate approach to administration (Kendig et al., 1996). Using a cut-off of 1 hour, 'delays' in prophylactic administration were noted for 1 in 3 babies (Figure 8.1). This was in accord with the observation by the UK neonatal staffing study that surfactant was more likely to be administered within the first hour after delivery in well-staffed units of medium activity where guidelines stated that prophylaxis should be given as soon possible after birth (Tucker, 2002).

Should all babies born at 27–28 weeks have received prophylactic surfactant? Such a policy would be easier to interpret and would prevent delays in administration. The benefits would be an improved survival rate and reduction in pneumothoraces. The systematic review on this subject (Soll and Morley, 2001) suggested a 40% reduction in mortality rate: applying this to the 117 deaths that were in the group that did not receive surfactant in the first hour of life suggests 47 babies would have survived. This calculation excludes the 19 babies who died within the first hour of life and whom the panels considered too ill to receive surfactant. However, it is likely to be an overestimate as the levels of antenatal steroid administration were higher in our study than in the systematic review. Despite this lack of accuracy there were at least two babies and probably more (Table 8.4) who died and should have received surfactant. Certainly for any baby who dies and has not received surfactant the reasons should be reviewed locally to ensure there was no failure of care.

It remains to be determined whether there is now enough evidence to recommend universal prophylactic administration of surfactant to babies born at 27–28 weeks gestation.

CONCLUSION

Surfactant therapy for babies born at 27–28 weeks gestation was overall of good standard. Most intubated babies (96%) received surfactant, but the timing of administration suggests that in only two-thirds was this given as soon as possible. Delays in administration were the most frequent concern of the panels, especially in the babies who died. The criteria for 'at risk of RDS' are uncertain. If a policy of administering surfactant to all babies within an hour of birth were implemented, an additional 12% of babies at this gestation would receive surfactant, and 1 in 3 babies would receive it substantially earlier. This is likely to afford a small but definite improvement in survival rates. A more explicit national recommendation about timing of administration is required, with guidance on whether this should be universal or selective.

RECOMMENDATIONS

At national and commissioning level

8.1 There should be guidance concerning the timing and gestation at which prophylactic surfactant should be administered and the indications for repeat doses.

At Trust level

Clinical practice

8.2 Surfactant replacement treatment should be readily available and given as soon as possible after intubation of infants born at 27–28 weeks gestation.

Local guidelines

8.3 Units should ensure that there are guidelines for the use of surfactant, which should include time of administration, preparation, dosage and the gestational range (upper and lower) during which surfactant should be given prophylactically.

Documentation and audit

8.4 Administration of surfactant should be documented, including dose, type, reasons for non-administration, timing of intubation and names of staff involved.

8.5 Surfactant administration should be audited. Failures and delays to administer surfactant to infants of 27–28 weeks gestation or less should be reviewed locally.

9
Ventilatory support

Most preterm infants born at 27–28 weeks gestation need some form of ventilatory support because of respiratory distress syndrome (RDS). The aim of ventilation in these babies is to achieve an adequate gas exchange without harmful side effects on pulmonary or cerebral function. This requires the provision of intensive care including regular monitoring of blood gas levels and responsive ventilation management (BAPM/RCPCH, 1992; RCPCH, 2000). The ventilatory support standard used for the Enquiry related to best practice (BAPM/RCPCH, 1992).

METHODS USED TO MONITOR BLOOD GASES

Blood gases were monitored for 327 (93%) babies who died and 385 (99%) babies who survived. They were not monitored for 26 babies: 25 deaths (19 of whom died during resuscitation) and 1 survivor. The methods are listed in Table 9.1, the commonest being by intermittent arterial blood sampling via an indwelling cannula or catheter (71%, 506/712) or pulse oximetry (71%, 503/712). Pulse oximetry was used alone in 7 cases, intermittent arterial puncture alone in 2 cases, capillary sample alone in 27 cases (11 deaths). Transcutaneous monitoring was never used alone.

Table 9.1   Methods used to monitor blood gases

	Babies who died (%)[a] n = 366		Babies who survived (%)[a] n = 395	
Intermittent arterial blood sampling via an indwelling cannula or catheter at any stage	242	(74.0)	264	(68.6)
Used alone	42		48	
Pulse oximetry at any stage	229	(70.0)	274	(71.2)
Used alone	5		2	
Capillary samples at any stage	131	(40.1)	187	(48.6)
Used alone	11		16	
Indwelling (arterial) electrode at any stage	58	(17.7)	50	(13.0)
Used alone	6		12	
Transcutaneous pO_2 at any stage	56	(17.1)	48	(12.5)
Used alone	0		0	
Intermittent arterial blood gas via arterial puncture	23	(7.0)	29	(7.5)
Used alone	2		0	
[Data missing]	39		10	

[a]   The percentage was calculated from the number of babies for which the information was provided.

STANDARD: VENTILATORY SUPPORT

The standard for neonatal ventilatory support was in three parts.

> **STANDARDS FOR VENTILATORY SUPPORT**
>
> **a** Regular blood gas analysis should be performed whilst the infant remains ventilated, on CPAP or in supplementary oxygen (BAPM/RCPCH, 1992)
>
> **b** Ventilation should be adjusted with the aim of maintaining a pH >7.25 and PaO_2 6–10 kPa (BAPM/RCPCH, 1992)
>
> **c** The response to therapy should be clearly recorded along with the remedial action taken (Project 27/28 Working Group; CESDI 6th Annual Report, 1999)

Panels were asked to assess whether the overall efforts to achieve this standard were good, fair or poor (Table 9.2). Failure to meet the standard was defined as poor effort. This was noted in 18 % of the babies who died and 7% of the babies who survived. This difference was statistically significant.

Table 9.2 Standard: efforts to meet the standard of ventilatory support

	Babies who died (%) [a] n = 366	Babies who survived (%) [a] n = 395	Crude OR (95% CI) p value	Adjusted [b] OR (95% CI) p value
Good	173 (47.3)	281 (71.1) ⎱	Reference group	Reference group
Fair	86 (23.5)	69 (17.5) ⎰		
Poor	65 (17.8)	28 (7.1)	3.14 (1.96–5.03) <0.001 [c]	3.29 (1.97–5.49) <0.001 [c]
Not relevant	33	11		
[Data missing]	9	6		

[a] The percentage was calculated from the number of babies for which the information was provided.
[b] Adjusted for sex, birthweight ≤5th centile and condition of baby at 5 minutes of age.
[c] Good or Fair vs Poor

PANEL OPINION

Some aspects of ventilatory support were considered deficient in 50% of the babies who died and in 34% of those who survived. This difference was statistically significant (Table 9.3).

Table 9.3 Panel opinion: ventilatory support

	Babies who died (%) [a] n = 366	Babies who survived (%) [a] n = 395	Crude OR (95% CI) p value	Adjusted [b] OR (95% CI) p value
Deficiencies in ventilatory support	167 (49.6)	132 (33.9)	1.91 (1.4–2.61) <0.001	2.08 (1.49–2.90) <0.001
[Data missing]	29	6		

[a] The percentage was calculated from the number of babies for which the information was provided.
[b] Adjusted for sex, birthweight ≤5th centile and condition of baby at 5 minutes of age.

The panels made 540 comments on these deficiencies: 302 comments related to 167 (50%) babies who died and 238 to 132 (34%) babies who survived. These are categorised in Table 9.4.

Table 9.4 Ventilatory support: number of comments and percentage of babies involved

	Babies who died n = 366		Babies who survived n = 395	
	Number of comments	Number and (%)[a] of babies n = 337	Number of comments	Number and (%)[a] of babies n = 389
Inadequate ventilation	138	99 (29.4)	134	93 (23.9)
Lack of management plan	37		22	
Failure or delay in responding to blood gas	31		21	
Overventilation/hypocarbia[b]	22		35	
Inappropriate ventilator settings	20		14	
Delay in intubation/ventilation	12		9	
Extubation/weaning too early	8		5	
Documented hyperoxaemia[c]	5		8	
Delay in weaning	3		20	
Lack of appropriate monitoring	52	52 (15.4)	37	37 (9.5)
Poor blood gas monitoring	47		33	
Lack of transcutaneous monitoring (TcPO$_2$)	5		4	
Poor documentation	34	34 (10.1)	23	23 (5.9)
Endotracheal tube problems	25	25 (7.4)	15	15 (3.9)
Malposition	9		7	
Multiple attempts at intubation	6		3	
Failed intubation	4		1	
Incorrect size	3		1	
Accidental extubation	3		1	
Other	0		2	
Poor management of complications	12	12 (3.6)	3	3 (0.8)
Pneumothorax	10		3	
Pulmonary haemorrhage	2		0	
Intra-arterial access failure	10	10 (3.0)	11	11 (2.8)
Drug administration issues	7	7 (2.1)	7	7 (1.8)
Surfactant	6		4	
Other	1		3	
Chest X ray misinterpreted	7	7 (2.1)	2	2 (0.5)
Lack of senior staff supervision	6	6 (1.8)	5	6 (1.3)
Problems during transfer	3	3 (0.9)	0	0
Miscellaneous	8	8 (2.4)	1	1 (0.3)
Any failure	302	167 (49.6)	238	132 (33.9)

[a]   The percentage was calculated from the number of babies for which an opinion was provided.
[b]   When documented in comments $PaCO_2$ values were <3.5 kPa.
[c]   When documented in comments PaO_2 values were >13 kPa.

DISCUSSION

Of all the babies in the study, 83% required ventilatory support on admission to the neonatal unit. It was of concern that there was a marked difference in the levels of effort made to achieve the standard in the care of the babies who died compared with the care of those that survived (Table 9.2). The panels' chief concern was a series of issues relating to poor ventilation technique, notably:

- a lack of management plan
- delays or failures in responding to blood gas results
- inappropriate ventilator settings.

Less common but still more frequently noted in the babies who died were endotracheal tube problems and poor management of complications such as pneumothorax.

Superficially this suggests that the quality of ventilatory care was in part responsible for the outcome. However, two reservations must be made before this conclusion can be accepted.

- First, critically ill babies are more difficult to manage. To allow for this in the comparison an adjustment was made for condition of the baby at 5 minutes of age as a marker of illness severity. After adjustment, there were only minor changes in odds ratios of the association between standard or panel opinion of ventilatory support and death.

- Second, appraising ventilatory support was particularly problematic, as no strong evidence-based or easily measurable criteria are available. The standards were defined by accepted best practice (BAPM, 1999; RCPCH, 2000) and their assessment was subjective. It is possible that as the assessors were aware of the outcome this may have influenced their assessment. This awareness may also have led to a more diligent itemising of substandard care in the babies who died.

Paradoxically there were two particular criticisms that were more frequently associated with survival than with death: overventilation and delay in ventilation weaning which can lead to excessively low PCO_2 or hyperoxaemia. Because a significant proportion of the babies died within the first 24 hours there would have been less opportunity to overventilate or delay weaning, partly explaining the difference observed. Hypocarbia reduces cerebral blood flow and may be associated with an increased risk of long-term neurodevelopmental problems (Dammann et al., 2001). However, these outcomes were not part of the Enquiry, so this observation in nearly 10% of the babies who survived remains an area of concern.

CONCLUSIONS

Ventilation support was considered to be good for 71% of the babies who survived. Despite this, ventilatory care received more panel comments than any other neonatal aspect of the Enquiry. The main issues related to lack of management plans and failure to respond to blood gas analysis. More deficiencies were identified in the babies who died (50%) than in the babies who survived (34%). This difference was still significant after allowing for the severity of illness of the baby shortly after birth.

Clear management guidelines and better staff training might increase the survival of preterm babies at 27–28 weeks gestation.

RECOMMENDATIONS

Terms indicated in **bold** are defined in the Glossary (p. xv).

At Trust level

Training

9.1 All staff involved in the provision of respiratory support for a baby born at 27–28 weeks gestation should have received training in airway management and ventilatory support. This should include all modes and types of ventilation and interpretation of gas analysis.

Clinical practice

9.2 Blood gas monitoring should be performed whilst the infant remains ventilated, on CPAP, or in supplementary oxygen, and the results recorded. Responses should be consistent with local guidelines.

9.3 Arterial cannulation should be attempted in all infants born at 27–28 weeks gestation requiring **intensive care.**

9.4 Intubation and reintubation of infants born at 27–28 weeks gestation should be supervised or undertaken by trained staff who are immediately available at all times.

Local guidelines

9.5 Units that manage infants born at 27–28 weeks gestation should have guidelines for:

- all modes and types of ventilation in use in the unit
- the criteria for artificial ventilation including the policy for infants on nasal CPAP and monitoring procedures to avoid inappropriately high or low PO_2 and PCO_2 concentrations.

Documentation and audit

9.6 Documentation should include timing of the first blood gas sample (apart from the cord blood gas), blood gas results, treatment changes and responses to treatment.

9.7 Units should identify and review problems in ventilated infants, in particular accidental extubation and pneumothorax.

10 *Cardiovascular support*

Neonatal intensive care aims at maintaining appropriate tissue perfusion. This in turn depends on cardiac output, blood pressure and peripheral vascular resistance (Weindling and Kissack, 2001). Low blood pressure and low blood flow are associated with peri/intraventricular haemorrhage (P/IVH), ischaemic cerebral lesions, poor long-term neurodevelopmental outcome and mortality in the preterm infant (Osborn and Evans, 2001). Good clinical practice includes measurement of blood pressure and prompt treatment of hypotension when it is accompanied by evidence of poor perfusion (BAPM, 1999).

The panels were asked to identify the methods used to monitor blood pressure and the actions taken to maintain blood pressure. They also assessed a standard relating to best practice (BAPM, 1999) and identified deficiencies of cardiovascular support in the first 7 days of care.

METHODS USED TO MONITOR BLOOD PRESSURE

Blood pressure was known to be monitored for 550 babies (256 deaths and 294 survivors). It was not monitored for 24 babies (all deaths), 22 of whom died during resuscitation.

Monitoring methods are listed in Table 10.1. Blood pressure monitoring using an indwelling cannula was used at some stage for 82% of babies who died and 71% of babies who survived.

MEAN ARTERIAL BLOOD PRESSURE VALUES

The lowest mean arterial blood pressure recorded in the first 12 hours was information the panels were asked to fill in. Values ranged between 10 and 64 mmHg. The lowest mean arterial blood pressure among the babies in the study was 27.1 mmHg (95% CI 26.4–27.9) at 27 weeks gestation and

29.2 mmHg (95% CI 28.4–29.9) at 28 weeks gestation. This was a significant difference (p < 0.001).

At each gestation, the lowest mean arterial blood pressure was also significantly lower in the babies who died (Figure 10.1). At 27 weeks the lowest mean arterial blood pressure was 25.5 mmHg (95% CI 24.4–26.5) in the babies who died and 28.5 mmHg (95% CI 27.6–29.5) in the survivors (p < 0.001). At 28 weeks the lowest mean arterial blood pressure was 28.1 mmHg (95% CI 27.1–29.1) in the babies who died and 30.1 mmHg (95% CI 29.0–31.1) in the survivors (p < 0.01).

Table 10.1   Methods used to monitor blood pressure

	Babies who died (%)[a] n = 366	Babies who survived (%)[a] n = 395
Invasive		
Indwelling cannula at any stage	210/256 (82)	209/294 (71.1)
Non-invasive		
Dinamap at any stage	81/256 (31.6)	112/294 (38.1)
Doppler at any stage	20/256 (7.8)	15/294 (5.1)

[a]   The percentage was calculated from the number of babies for which the information was available.

Figure 10.1   Lowest mean arterial blood pressure in first 12 hours of life by gestation and survival status

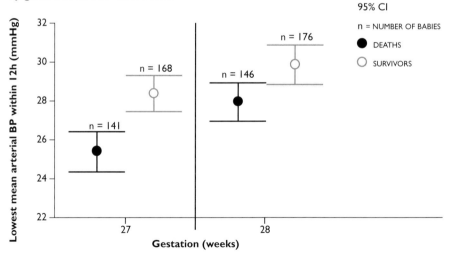

ACTION TAKEN TO MAINTAIN BLOOD PRESSURE

The panels were asked to indicate what action was taken to maintain blood pressure independent of the baby's blood pressure status.

Some action to maintain blood pressure was taken in 80% of babies who died and 50% of babies who survived. Babies who died were significantly more likely to require action than those who survived (Table 10.2). These actions comprised volume expansion (34%), inotropic drugs (8%) or a combination of both (39%).

Table 10.2   Action taken to maintain blood pressure

	Babies who died (%)[a] n = 366	Babies who survived (%)[a] n = 395	OR (95% CI) p value
None	63 (19.2)	183 (50.4)	Reference group
Volume expansion	111 (33.8)	109 (30.0)	4.28 (3.03–6.03) <0.001[b]
Volume expansion and inotropic drugs	128 (39.0)	57 (15.7)	4.28 (3.03–6.03) <0.001[b]
Inotropic drugs	26 (7.9)	14 (3.9)	4.28 (3.03–6.03) <0.001[b]
[Data missing]	38	32	

[a]   The percentage was calculated from the number of babies for which the information was provided.
[b]   None vs volume expansion and/or inotropic drugs.

STANDARD: CARDIOVASCULAR SUPPORT

The standard for cardiovascular support was in three parts.

> **STANDARD FOR CARDIOVASCULAR SUPPORT**
>
> **a**   Blood pressure should be monitored regularly while the infant remains unwell (BAPM, 1999)
>
> **b**   The mean blood pressure (mmHg) should be managed with the aim of maintaining it at or above the infant's gestation in weeks (BAPM, 1999)
>
> **c**   The response to therapy should be clearly recorded along with remedial action taken (Project 27/28 Working Group; CESDI 6th Annual Report, 1999)

The panels were asked to indicate whether they thought the efforts made to achieve the standard were good, fair or poor (Table 10.3) and to identify cases not relevant to this standard. Failure to meet the standard of cardiovascular support was defined as a poor effort. This was noted in 15% of the babies who died and 7% of the babies who survived. This difference was statistically significant (Table 10.3).

Table 10.3 Standard: efforts to meet the standard of cardiovascular support

	Babies who died (%)[a] n = 366	Babies who survived (%)[a] n = 395	OR (95% CI) p value	Adjusted[b] OR (95% CI) p value
Good	203 (65.3)	269 (77.3)	Reference group	Reference group
Fair	62 (19.9)	56 (16.1)		
Poor	46 (14.8)	23 (6.6)	2.45 (1.45–4.15)	2.37 (1.36–4.13)
Not relevant	48	43	0.001[c]	0.002[c]
[Data missing]	7	4		

[a] The percentage was calculated from the number of babies for which the information was provided.
[b] Adjusted for sex, birthweight ≤5th centile and condition of baby at 5 minutes of age.
[c] Good or Fair vs Poor

PANEL OPINION

Some aspect of cardiovascular support was considered deficient in 34% of the babies who died and 20% of the babies who survived. This difference was statistically significant (Table 10.4).

Table 10.4 Panel opinion: cardiovascular support

	Babies who died (%)[a] n = 366	Babies who survived (%)[a] n = 395	OR (95% CI) p value	Adjusted[b] OR (95% CI) p value
Deficiencies in cardiovascular support	102 (33.5)	67 (19.7)	2.06 (1.44–2.95) <0.001	2.13 (1.45–3.15) <0.001
[Data missing]	62	54		

[a] The percentage was calculated from the number of babies for which the information was provided.
[b] Adjusted for sex, birthweight ≤5th centile and condition of baby at 5 minutes of age.

The panels made 232 comments on these deficiencies: 141 of them related to 102 (34%) babies who died and 91 to 67 (20%) babies who survived. The comments are categorised in Table 10.5.

Table 10.5 Cardiovascular support: number of comments and percentage of babies involved

	Babies who died n = 366		Babies who survived n = 395	
	Number of comments	Number and (%) ^{a} of babies n = 304	Number of comments	Number and (%) ^{a} of babies n = 340
Treatment deficiencies	72	61 (20.1)	34	25 (7.4)
No inotropes administered or delay in their use	19		9	
Excessive intravenous fluids given	13		6	
Inappropriate use of drugs	12		4	
Drug errors	8		2	
No blood transfusion administered	8		2	
No fluid bolus administered	7		6	
No or delayed treatment	5		5	
Documentation	23	23 (7.6)	22	22 (6.5)
BP not documented	11		17	
Other issues	12		5	
Poor assessment of cardiovascular function	26	26 (8.6)	17	17 (5.0)
Poor monitoring of blood pressure	16		14	
Failure to recognise cause of hypotension	6		1	
Incomplete assessment	2		1	
Failure to perform echocardiogram	2		1	
Intravenous access issues	9	8 (2.6)	6	6 (1.8)
No or delayed central access	7		6	
Inadequate intravenous access	2		0	
Miscellaneous	11	11(3.6)	12	12 (3.5)
Any failure	141	102 (33.5)	91	67 (19.7)

^{a} The percentage was calculated from the number of babies for which the information was provided.

DISCUSSION

Cardiovascular support is essential for the management of preterm infants, especially critically ill infants. It includes both the measurement of blood pressure and prompt treatment of hypotension accompanied by evidence of poor perfusion. Poor efforts at achieving cardiovascular support were twice as likely to occur in babies who died as in those who survived.

To what degree do these failures contribute directly to the death of the baby, or are they influenced by the degree of illness in the baby or panel opinion? Certainly critically ill babies are more difficult to support, and their hypotension may be more resistant to treatment. To allow for this, an adjustment was made allowing for the condition of the baby at 5 minutes of age as a marker of illness severity. After adjusting for condition of the baby, the association between poor standard of care and death remained. Failures of care may also have been more readily assigned when the panel was aware of the outcome for the baby. This is especially so when the standard is subjective, as was the case for cardiovascular support where it was dependent on appraising efforts made. Notwithstanding these considerations, it remains likely that poor cardiovascular support contributed to some of the deaths.

Although it was not a prime objective of the Enquiry to define acceptable limits for blood pressure, it provided data from a large number of babies. There is no agreed definition of hypotension in newborn babies, and blood pressure level correlates with gestational and postnatal age. A commonly used and practical working definition of hypotension is that mean blood pressure in millimetres of mercury (MBP) is below the value of the gestational age in weeks (BAPM/RCPCH, 1992). However, this is based on a small study of 16 relatively stable babies weighing less than 1 kg (Versmold et al., 1981; BAPM, 1999).

Two-thirds of babies underwent some intervention to maintain their blood pressure within the first 7 days of life. Deficiencies in care were noted in a third of the babies who died and in a fifth of the babies who survived. The two most frequent concerns were failure or delays in administering inotropes, and excessive intravenous fluids.

First line treatment for hypotension is volume expansion (10–20 ml/kg) (BAPM, 1999). The Enquiry did not assess the type of volume expansion but current evidence suggests that saline is as effective as plasma in increasing the blood pressure (RCPCH, 2000). Repeated volume expansion is counterproductive unless there is clear evidence of hypovolaemia, massive capillary leak or blood loss (BAPM, 1999). A regional study based on this Enquiry found that excessive volume expansion might be associated with an increased risk of death in preterm babies born at 27–28 weeks gestation (Ewer et al., in press).

Second line treatment consists of inotropic support (BAPM, 1999), commonly dopamine or dobutamine. Dopamine has a vasoconstrictor effect and doses above 15 µg/kg per minute increase pulmonary vascular resistance and are not recommended. Comments did not favour any particular inotropes. However, recent work has demonstrated dopamine to be more effective than dobutamine in increasing the MBP (RCPCH, 2000; Subhedar and Shaw, 2001).

Problems with assessment of cardiovascular function were identified in 9% of babies who died and 5% of babies who survived. Intravascular monitoring via a catheter or a cannula is the most accurate and reliable way of recording blood pressure in the sick neonate (BAPM, 1999), and was used in 82% of the babies who died and 71% of those who survived. Non-invasive oscillometric monitoring (Dinamap) is easy to use and safe in stable babies but may overestimate MBP by 5–10 mmHg and may fail to identify transient hypotension or unstable blood pressure as effectively as invasive monitoring (Low et al., 1995). Failures here contribute to delays in responding to hypotensive episodes.

CONCLUSION

Cardiovascular support was considered good for 65% of babies who died and 77% of babies who survived. More deficiencies were identified in the babies who died (34%) than in the babies who survived (20%). This difference was still significant after allowing for the severity of illness of the baby shortly after birth. The most frequent concern was the delay or failure to use inotropes. Particular attention is required to ensuring a timely response to hypotension and correct application of inotropic support.

RECOMMENDATIONS

Terms indicated in **bold** are defined in the Glossary (p. xv).

At Trust level

Clinical practice

10.1 Every attempt should be made to monitor blood pressure continuously in infants born at 27–28 weeks gestation, undergoing **intensive care** using an indwelling arterial catheter.

10.2 Inotropes should be administered to infants who remain hypotensive after cautious volume expansion (not more than 20 ml/kg) and in the absence of specific hypovolaemic conditions causing hypotension (e.g. haemorrhage).

Local guidelines

10.3 Units should have guidelines for:

- monitoring of cardiovascular status, including indications for intravascular monitoring and recording requirements
- the use of volume expansion, including indications and maximum volumes
- the use of inotropes, including indications and dose schedules.

Management of infection

Preterm babies, especially those below 28 weeks gestation, are at increased risk of infection. This can be due to a maternal infection that may have triggered the preterm labour. Other factors include immaturity of the immune system and the invasive procedures required in neonatal intensive care (Hall and Ironton, 1999). The incidence of sepsis in babies whose birthweight is around 1 kg varies between 15% and 25%, with an associated mortality of around 20% (Vermont-Oxford 1993; Hall and Ironton, 1999).

The Enquiry assessed early management of infection (screening and antibiotic therapy) on admission to the neonatal unit and later management during the first week of life. There are no established standards or national recommendations for this topic (BAPM, 1999; RCPCH, 2000).

EARLY MANAGEMENT OF INFECTION

Maternal temperature and cultures prior to delivery; blood cultures in babies on admission

There was no significant difference in mean maternal temperature for babies who died (36.9°C ±0.6 SD) or survived (37.0°C ±0.6 SD) (p = 0.14).

A positive maternal culture occurred in 15% of babies who died (45/307) and in 16% (57/352) of babies who survived (Table 11.1). The commonest organisms in the maternal cultures were group B streptococcus (30%), candida (15%) and coliforms (11%).

Blood cultures were less likely to be taken from babies who died (88%; 296/338) than from babies who survived (98%; 373/381) (p < 0.001). A positive blood culture was observed significantly more frequently in the babies who died (15%; 39/262) than in those who survived (8%; 29/351) (Table 11.1).

Table 11.1 Cultures in mothers and babies

	Babies who died (%) [a] n = 366	Babies who survived (%) [a] n = 395	Crude OR (95% C I) p value
Positive maternal culture	45/307 (14.7)	57/352 (16.2)	0.86 (0.55–1.35) 0.59
Blood culture taken in baby	296/338 (87.6)	373/381 (97.9)	6.62 (3.06–14.31) <0.001
Positive blood culture	39/262 (14.9)	29/351 (8.3)	1.94 (1.17–3.23) <0.02

[a] The percentage was calculated from the number of babies for which the information was provided.

Most positive blood cultures were *Escherichia coli* (15%) and Group B streptococcus (8%) (Table 11.2).

Table 11.2 Results of initial blood culture in babies

Pathogen	Babies who died (%) [a] n = 39	Babies who survived (%) [a] n = 29
E. coli	8 (21.0)	2 (7.1)
Staphylococcus epidermidis/contaminant	7 (18.4)	11 (39.3)
Group B Streptococcus	5 (13.1)	0
Enterobacter cloacae	3 (7.9)	0
Mixed growth/contaminant	3 (7.9)	1 (3.6)
Diphtheroids	2 (5.3)	2 (7.1)
Pseudomonas	2 (5.3)	0
Staphylococcus aureus	1 (2.6)	1 (3.6)
Haemophilus influenzae	0	1 (3.6)
Serratia	0	1 (3.6)
Streptococcus pneumoniae	0	1 (3.6)
Other [b]	7 (18.4)	8 (28.6)
[Data missing]	1	1

[a] The percentage was calculated from the number of babies for which the information was provided.

[b] This group consisted mainly of contaminants and included Bacillus, Corynebacterium, gram-positive cocci, coliforms, enterococci, Stenotrophomonas, Streptococcus oralis, Streptococcus mitis, Staphylococcus, Streptococcus sanguinis and Propionobacter.

Initial antibiotic treatment of babies

Most babies were commenced on antibiotics on admission to the neonatal unit: 87% (305/350) of babies who died and 97% (379/391) of survivors. There was no difference in the median time after admission that antibiotics were commenced between babies who died (2 hours, interquartile range [IQR] 1–3) and survivors (2 hours, IQR 1–3) (p = 0.99, Mann–Whitney test).

The median length of antibiotic treatment for the babies who died was 3 days (IQR 6–5) and 5 days (IQR 3–6) for the survivors (p < 0.001, Mann–Whitney test). The duration of antibiotic treatment was ≤ 7 days in 97% of cases.

Panel opinion

Some aspect of the early management of infection was considered deficient in 20% (70/346) of babies who died and 16% (63/393) of the babies who survived (Table 11.3).

Table 11.3 Panel opinion: early management of infection

	Babies who died (%)[a] n = 366	Babies who survived (%)[a] n = 395	OR (95% CI) p value	Adjusted[b] OR (95% CI) p value
Deficiencies in early management	70 (20.2)	63 (16.0)	1.33 (0.91–1.93) 0.14	1.32 (0.87–2.0) 0.19
[Data missing]	20	2		

[a] The percentage was calculated from the number of babies for which the information was provided.
[b] Adjusted for sex, birthweight ≤5th centile and condition of baby at 5 minutes of age.

The panels made 149 comments on these deficiencies: 77 comments related to 70 (20%) babies who died and 72 to 63 (16%) babies who survived. These are categorised in Table 11.4.

LATER MANAGEMENT OF INFECTION

Subsequent blood cultures in addition to those taken on admission to the neonatal unit were taken in the first week in 41% (147/361) of babies who survived and 40% (100/252) of babies who died. Information about these blood cultures being taken was missing for 34 babies who survived and 35 babies who died, and not applicable for 79 babies who died. Among these 79 there were 54 babies who died in the first 24 hours of life for whom data was classified by panels as not applicable. Most of the later blood cultures were taken because of clinical deterioration or suspected sepsis (66%) or necrotising enterocolitis (22%).

Antibiotic choice varied considerably, the most common being a combination of penicillins and aminoglycosides. Seven types of antibiotics were used in combination or alone: penicillins, aminoglycosides, cephalosporins, metronidazole, teicoplanin, macrolide and antiviral.

Most repeat blood culture results were negative. Amongst positives, *Staphylococcus epidermidis* was the most reported organism (Table 11.5).

Table 11.4 Early management of infection: number of comments and percentage of babies involved

	Babies who died n = 366		Babies who survived n = 395	
	Number of comments	Number and (%) [a] of babies n = 345	Number of comments	Number and (%) [a] of babies n = 392
Inappropriate antibiotic management	58	52 (15.1)	48	42 (10.7)
Delay in administering antibiotics	29		21	
Choice of antibiotics questioned	13		6	
Antibiotics not administered	8		5	
Failure to recognise underlying condition and change management accordingly	5		4	
Inappropriate continuation of antibiotics	2		7	
Drug errors	1		3	
Multiple antibiotic changes	1		0	
Inappropriate discontinuation of antibiotics	0		5	
Inappropriate screening for sepsis	9	9 (2.6)	9	9 (2.3)
Blood cultures not taken	5		5	
Lumbar puncture performed inappropriately	2		2	
Delay in taking blood cultures	1		0	
Lumbar puncture not performed	1		2	
Miscellaneous	7	7 (2.0)	8	8 (2.0)
Documentation	3	3 (0.9)	3	3 (0.8)
Central access issues	0	0	4	4 (1.0)
Any failures	77	70 (20.2)	72	63 (16.0)

[a] The percentage was calculated from the number of babies for which an opinion was provided.

Table 11.5   Results of repeated blood culture taken from babies during the first week of life

Blood culture result	Babies who died (%) [a] n = 100	Babies who survived (%) [a] n = 147
No growth	47 (59.5)	79 (72.5)
S. epidermidis	17 (21.5)	24 (22.0)
S. aureus	2 (2.5)	1 (0.9)
E. coli	2 (2.5)	0
Group B streptococcus	2 (2.5)	0
Pseudomonas	2 (2.5)	0
E. cloacae	2 (2.5)	0
Klebsiella	1 (1.3)	1 (0.9)
MRSA [b]	1 (1.3)	0
Other	3 (3.8)	4 (3.7)
[Data missing]	21	38

[a]   The percentage was calculated from the number of babies for which the information was provided.
[b]   Methicillin-resistant S. aureus.

Panel opinion

Some aspect of the later management of infection was considered deficient in 15% (59/387) of the babies who survived and 15% (45/306) of the babies who died (Table 11.6). The large number of missing data included the babies who died early in the first week.

Table 11.6   Panel opinion: later management of infection

	Babies who died (%) [a] n = 366	Babies who survived (%) [a] n = 395	Crude OR (95% CI) p value	Adjusted [b] OR (95% CI) p value
Deficiencies in later management	45 (14.7)	59 (15.2)	0.96 (0.63–1.46) 0.84	1.21 (0.76–1.91) 0.42
[Data missing]	60	8		

[a]   The percentage was calculated from the number of babies for which the information was provided.
[b]   Adjusted for sex, birthweight ≤5th centile and condition of baby at 5 minutes of age.

The panels made 133 comments on these deficiencies: 61 comments related to 45 (15%) babies who died and 72 to 59 (15%) babies who survived. These are categorised in Table 11.7.

Table 11.7 Later management of infection: number of comments and percentage of babies involved

	Babies who died % n = 366		Babies who survived % n = 395	
	Number of comments	Number and (%)[a] of babies n = 306	Number of comments	Number and (%)[a] of babies n = 387
Inappropriate screening for sepsis	26	26 (8.5)	32	30 (7.8)
Failure to take blood cultures	22		23	
No infection screen	3		3	
Failure to perform lumbar puncture	1		5	
MRSA screen not performed	0		1	
Inappropriate antibiotic management	11	11 (3.6)	18	17 (4.4)
Choice of antibiotics queried	4		8	
Drug errors	2		0	
Failure to commence antibiotics	1		2	
Antibiotics should have been continued	1		1	
Antibiotics should have been discontinued	0		4	
Miscellaneous	3		3	
Assessment failures	14	11 (3.6)	4	4 (1.0)
Delayed intervention	11		1	
Failure to recognise signs of sepsis	3		3	
Documentation	4	4 (1.3)	11	11 (2.8)
Miscellaneous	6	6 (2.0)	7	7 (1.8)
Any failure	61	45 (15.0)	72	59 (15.0)

[a] The percentage was calculated from the number of babies for which the information was provided.

DISCUSSION

Most preterm babies of 27–28 weeks gestation are screened for sepsis and treated with antibiotics. Examples of inadequate management of infection were noted in 18% of babies on admission to the neonatal unit and in a further 15% of these babies during the first week of life, but these were not associated with deaths. These results should be interpreted with caution.

Elevated maternal temperature and positive maternal cultures were not associated with death of the babies. The common pathogens responsible for neonatal infections such as group B streptococcus and *E. coli* were also present in maternal cultures (Dear, 1999).

It is often difficult to differentiate respiratory distress syndrome (RDS) from early onset septicaemia due to group B streptococcus. For this reason the initial investigation of babies with RDS should include a blood culture (BAPM, 1999). Most babies (93%) in this Enquiry had blood taken for culture. The fact that fewer cultures were taken on admission from babies who died is attributable to early death rather than a failure of care, as was the shorter duration of antibiotic therapy in the death group.

A positive blood culture in the baby on admission to the neonatal unit was strongly associated with death. *E. coli* was the most frequently cultured pathogen, followed by group B streptococcus. However, it is difficult to comment on the prevalence of these organisms in maternal cultures and infant blood cultures in the general population because the focus on neonatal deaths at 27–28 weeks is likely to select a high proportion of cases of sepsis at birth. It is nevertheless important to note that the pathogens causing severe perinatal infections (Grauel et al., 1989; Dear, 1999) are most often found in the deaths group. A significant proportion of babies gave positive results due to likely contaminants (mixed growth and *S. epidermidis*): sterile precautions during technical procedures should be reinforced (Malathi, 1993).

Most neonatologists commence antibiotic therapy as soon as possible after admission and before laboratory confirmation that infection is present or absent (BAPM, 1999). However, it appears that some babies were started on antibiotics without a prior blood culture (684 babies started on antibiotics for 669 documented blood cultures). There were also 10 comments on blood cultures not taken when the panel thought they should have been.

A high proportion of babies (40%) had a repeat blood culture and this was negative in 67%. This confirms the awareness of staff to the risk of infection in preterm babies. *S. epidermidis* was the commonest organism cultured (22% of babies) in repeat blood culture. The other major pathogens noted were similar to those previously described.

Panels reported aspects of poor-quality care in equal proportion in deaths and survivors. The most frequent issue in early management of infection related to delays in administration of antibiotics. Subsequently the main problems were failures to screen for sepsis. Poor documentation was less frequent (1%) than in other aspects of the neonatal Enquiry.

CONCLUSION

Despite some deficiencies in screening and treatment of infection (most notably delay in administering antibiotics), there was a good overall standard in this area. Deficiencies did not seem to be associated with the death of the babies but were nevertheless frequent enough to deserve attention. National guidance might assist individual units in their policy for the screening and treatment of infection.

RECOMMENDATIONS

At Trust level

Clinical practice

11.1 Contamination should be minimised by careful preparation of the skin before a sample is taken for blood culture (Malathi et al., 1993).

Local guidelines

11.2 Units should have guidelines for:

- screening, diagnosis and treatment of chorioamnionitis (infection in labour)
- screening, diagnosis and treatment of group B haemolytic streptococcus
- antibiotic use specifying type and indications for starting and stopping.

12 *Organisation of care*

Today, a baby born at 27–28 weeks gestation is highly likely to survive; in contrast, babies born at the same gestation in 1987 had only a 50% chance of survival (Field et al., 1991). Much of this improvement is due to effective interventions, such as administration of corticosteroids to the mother or surfactant replacement therapy, or to skilled care at birth and refinement of intensive care techniques. The full range of resources for neonatal intensive care, especially staff and equipment, cannot be deployed at every maternity unit. Neonatal services have developed without strategic planning, and neonatal intensive care is practised at a wide range of hospitals. Some units specialise as referral centres with the infrastructure to support intensive care, whereas others elect not to provide such services, making alternative arrangements for the antenatal or postnatal transfer of women and their babies for intensive care.

Health professionals are continually balancing the need to achieve the best outcome for the mother and baby while minimising the risk and disruption to the family that may occur with transfers between hospitals. Deciding if, when and where to transfer the mother and her baby is integral to the care of these infants. In the present Enquiry a quarter of mothers were transferred before delivery, and in a fifth of these transfers the mother was in labour. One in ten of the babies in the Enquiry had a transfer in the first week of life.

This section addresses the organisational aspects of care to the mother and the baby. It does not include failures of individual practice.

ORGANISATION OF OBSTETRIC CARE

Panel opinion

Deficiencies in the organisation of obstetric care were identified in 19% of mothers of babies who died and in 22% of mothers of babies who survived. This difference was not statistically significant (Table 12.1).

Table 12.1   Panel opinion: organisation of obstetric care

	Mothers of babies who died (%) [a] n = 352	Mothers of babies who survived (%) [a] n = 371	Crude OR (95% CI) p value	Adjusted [b] OR (95% CI) p value
Deficiencies in organisation of obstetric care	66 (19.3)	79 (22.1)	0.84 (0.58–1.21) 0.36	0.83 (0.57–1.20) 0.32
[Data missing]	10	14		

[a] The percentage was calculated from the number of mothers for which information was provided.
[b] Adjusted for preterm labour and PROM.

Analysis of comments

The panels made 167 comments on deficiencies in organisation of obstetric care: 78 comments related to 66 (19.3%) mothers of babies who died and 89 to 79 (22.1%) mothers of babies who survived. These are categorised in Table 12.2.

The most frequent problem was gaining access to neonatal facilities before delivery. This included the shortage of intensive care cots and consequent difficulty in arranging in-utero transfer. Some of the transfers were deemed inappropriate, in that they occurred out of a centre that should have been able to deliver such care or were considered inappropriate geographically (see Chapter 13).

The second most frequent problem relates to staffing issues. These were related to circumstances at the time of labour rather than during the antenatal period and included too junior staff, inadequate staffing levels and difficulties contacting staff.

Problems relating to general facilities included access to operating theatres, particularly at times of simultaneous emergencies. Concerns regarding the organisation of antenatal care covered a wide spectrum of issues. Many were a result of poor communication between health professionals. These issues are further discussed in Chapter 15. The organisational failures in antenatal care implied a lack of continuity in overall responsibility. Non-attendance for antenatal appointments in particular was poorly managed. The miscellaneous category included problems of interfacing with support facilities, for example referral patterns from the Accident and Emergency department and links with Social Services.

CONCLUSIONS

Over the past 10 years there have been major changes in the delivery of services for neonatal intensive care. Yet despite recommendations in 1995 and 1996 from CSAG and BAPM, organisational deficiencies were still frequent in 1998–2000. The standards proposed by BAPM (2001) for hospitals providing neonatal intensive and high dependency care included the formation of managed clinical networks. It is strongly recommended that these networks should be introduced. This is likely to reduce the frustrations of health professionals and parents and yield further improvements in outcomes for premature babies.

RECOMMENDATIONS

- Terms indicated in **bold** are defined in the Glossary (p. xv). Recommendations relating to transfer and communication are given in Chapters 13 and 15 respectively.

At national and commissioning level

12.1 The Department of Health and the Welsh Assembly Government should support the establishment of **managed clinical networks**.

12.2 Commissioners should ensure that there are appropriate numbers of medical neonatal posts at senior level.

12.3 Commissioners should ensure that there are training and career opportunities for midwives, nurses and especially advanced neonatal nurse practitioners (Smith and Hall, in press).

12.4 Commissioners should work with Trusts to coordinate maternity and neonatal care and to minimise **inappropriate transfers** and referrals.

At Trust level

Training

12.5 All staff should be trained and be aware of local arrangements for simultaneous obstetric and neonatal emergencies.

12.6 All junior medical staff present at delivery should be supervised and receive training in resuscitation and the subsequent management of preterm babies born at 27–28 weeks gestation.

12.7 All midwifery, nursing and medical staff should have training in the use of **equipment** required for resuscitation, ventilation, cardiovascular support and blood gas analysis.

Staffing

12.8 The arrangements for staffing should be reviewed to ensure:

– Availability of midwifery staff to deal with an unanticipated preterm delivery and or simultaneous obstetric emergencies. This should be in accordance with RCOG/RCM standards (1999).

– The presence of two members of the neonatal medical or nursing staff, who are sufficiently trained and experienced to carry out resuscitation and stabilisation, at the delivery of a preterm infant.

– Early and close neonatal consultant supervision of care during the first 24 hours for a baby born at 27–28 weeks gestation.

Communication

12.9 There should be a system to identify non-attenders and mothers who are at risk of preterm delivery, with appropriate arrangements for follow-up.

12.10 Every Accident and Emergency department should, if appropriate, ensure fast tracking of pregnant women to an obstetric opinion, even if maternity care is not the prime reason for attendance.

Local guidelines

12.12 There should be written policies for the maintenance, replacement and upgrading of **equipment** necessary for the support of the preterm baby. These should be consistent with the standards outlined by BAPM (2001).

Documentation and audit

12.13 Untoward incidents and drug errors should be reported and regularly audited, including the results of interventions and strategies to minimise these events.

For general documentation recommendations see Chapter 15.

13 Transfers before and after delivery

Neonatal intensive care is a high-cost, low-volume service that is not available at every maternity unit. If possible, babies should be born at units with appropriate facilities but since this cannot always be predicted, it is essential that there should be an efficient and safe system for transferring mothers and babies. A transfer prior to delivery (i.e. in-utero) is usually easier and safer for the baby, but may be inappropriate because of the mother's condition or the imminence of delivery. In these circumstances it may be more relevant to transfer after delivery (i.e. ex-utero). Regardless of timing, all types of transfers add to the anxiety and the financial costs for the supporting family.

In 1998–2000 most babies (3233/3522; 92%) born at 27–28 weeks gestation were born in a hospital providing neonatal intensive care. The notification system used in Project 27/28 did not identify transfers before birth but recorded 854 ex-utero transfers (i.e. 24% of babies) within the first 28 days of life. (CESDI 8th Annual Report, 2001).

This chapter summarises the enquiry findings concerning the care associated with both in-utero and ex-utero transfers. No formal standards were provided for the panels.

IN-UTERO TRANSFERS

Before delivery 26% (190/723) of mothers (92/352 of mothers of babies who died and 98/371 of mothers of babies who survived) were transferred (Table 13.1). The transfer occurred before labour for 19% (137) and in labour for 5% (38); no information was available for 2% (15). The in-utero transfers were characterised according to type of neonatal unit (as defined in Chapter 2) prior to transfer and at birth; transfer times; seniority of obstetrician involved in the decision to transfer; and indications for transfer.

The characteristics were similar for the mothers of babies who died and mothers of babies who survived (Table 13.1).

The indications for transfer in the mothers of babies who died were:

- inappropriate facilities for the mother and baby in the transferring hospital (46/87; 53%)
- a resource problem at the transferring hospital (34/87; 39%)
- other reasons (7/87; 8%) (Table 13.1).

In the cases of the mothers of babies who died the transferring hospital was:

- a unit routinely accepting referrals at this gestation (28/91; 31%)
- a unit which would routinely manage this gestation in-house (27/91; 29.7%)
- a unit without neonatal facilities (36/91; 40%) (Table 13.1).

A consultant obstetrician was involved in the decision to transfer in 77% of the mothers of babies who died. There were two cases (in both of which the baby survived) in which a senior house officer was the most senior obstetrician involved in the decision to transfer (Table 13.1).

In the mothers of babies who died the median decision-to-arrival time was 120 minutes and the median leaving-to-arrival time was 48 minutes (Table 13.1). These times were shorter than those reported for the mothers of babies who survived, but the difference was not statistically significant.

Panel opinion

Panels addressed three questions:

- If there was no transfer prior to delivery, should there have been?
- If there was a transfer, was the decision appropriate?
- Was the process of transfer satisfactory?

A transfer before delivery should have occurred in 5% (26/553) of cases in which the mother was not transferred (Table 13.2). Although numbers were small, deaths were particularly frequent in this group.

POSTMORTEM EXAMINATIONS

General aspects

Postmortem examination was discussed with the family in at least 75% of babies who died and 132 of 366 (36%) of these babies underwent a postmortem examination: 88% of these were full examinations and 12% were limited. In 94 cases it was possible to determine whether the postmortem had been carried out by a specialist perinatal pathologist. A specialist pathologist had performed 77% of these examinations. Panels identified deficiencies in 18% of specialist postmortem reports, compared with 60% of reports prepared by general pathologists (OR 7.04; 95% CI 2.4–20.7; $p < 0.001$). In 18% of reports seen by panels the histology was not available and in 4% the pathologist offered no diagnosis. Other deficiencies included lack of clinicopathological summary, incomplete macroscopic description and absence of a report on the placenta. A number of reports had multiple deficiencies. In addition, in four cases the significance of findings described in the report was overlooked (Table 14.2). Four cases highlighted the problems faced in some areas in providing a specialist perinatal pathology service: for two there was an excessive delay between death and postmortem (8 and 18 days), and the examination of a pair of twins was commenced by a local pathologist and subsequently transferred to a specialist.

Table 14.2 Findings overlooked by pathologist

Missed pulmonary hypoplasia

Missed significance of pericardial effusion

Failed to recognise significance of high liver/brain weight ratio and small thymus

Failed to recognise significance of positive blood culture result and formed inappropriate conclusion

In 45 cases panels identified discrepancies between the clinical assessment and the postmortem findings. Some of these were relatively minor, for example identification of intact subcapsular haematoma of the liver or minor germinal layer haemorrhage in the brain. Other more major discrepancies included identification of unsuspected pulmonary hypoplasia, refuted diagnosis of pulmonary hypoplasia, absence of suspected congenital malformation, myocardial infarction and identification of a torn velamentous blood vessel in the placenta (Table 14.3).

Table 14.3 Discrepancy between clinical assessment and postmortem findings

Condition	Discrepancy/Comment	Number of comments
Pulmonary hypoplasia	Identified at PM, not clinically	2
	Not confirmed at PM	4
Sepsis or NEC	Identified at PM, not clinically	6
	Not confirmed at PM	4
Intracerebral haemorrhage or hypoxic-ischaemic injury	Identified at PM, not clinically	6
	Not confirmed at PM	2
Growth or gestation	Reassessed by PM	3
Congenital anomaly	Not confirmed at PM	3
Pulmonary haemorrhage	Identified at PM, not clinically	3
Subcapsular haemorrhage of liver	Identified at PM, not clinically	3
Placental factors	Hydrops due to FMH	1
	Torn velamentous vessels	1
	Chorioamnionitis	1
Pulmonary pathology	BPD as cause of death	1
	HMD identified	1
Other	Myocardial infarction	1
	No lung aeration	1
	Renal disorder	1
	Hydronephrosis	1

BPD, bronchopulmonary dysplasia; FMH, fetal-maternal hemorrhage; HMD, hyaline membrane disease; NEC, necrotising enterocolitis; PM, postmortem.

Specific pathology

Lungs

The types of lung pathology identified were typical of extremely premature babies. In 10% the only abnormality was immaturity. This is in contrast with the clinical assessment provided on the rapid report forms (CESDI 8th Annual Report, 2001) which classified 26% as pulmonary immaturity. Pulmonary hypoplasia was identified in 13%, a very similar figure to the 15% given in the original paper by Wigglesworth et al. (1981). Hyaline membrane disease was found in 54% and chronic lung disease in 13%. Major pulmonary haemorrhage was present in 25% and pneumonia in 18%. Other potentially significant findings included pneumothorax (7.4%), interstitial emphysema (12.4%), pleural effusion/hydrops, herpes infection and pulmonary hypertension.

Brain

In only 62% of postmortem examination was brain histology available. Germinal layer and intraventricular haemorrhage was present in 43 (32.5%) of autopsies of which 24 were minor and 13 major (the remainder were not described). Hypoxic-ischaemic neuronal injury was identified in 20 cases, of which 8 were relatively mild or focal and 8 were severe or widespread. Periventricular leukomalacia was present in 9 cases and in 7 it was severe. Additional findings included cerebral oedema, cerebellar and subdural haemorrhages, dilated ventricles and a torn falx cerebri.

PANEL COMMENTS ON CONSENT AND DOCUMENTATION

Panel comments on consent and documentation of postmortem examination were identified in the different maternal, neonatal and general sections of the Enquiry. Consent issues were identified in 10 neonatal deaths. These were predominantly failure to offer postmortem examination to the family, when there were clear areas of uncertainty that might have been resolved by autopsy. In several cases postmortem examination appeared only to have been discussed with the family by a senior house officer or other inappropriately junior doctor. Documentation of the discussion relating to postmortem examination consent was felt to be poor in 6 cases and in a further 5 the case notes did not include any reference to the postmortem examination findings, even though they contradicted the clinical diagnosis. The reason for an apparently inappropriate referral to the coroner was not recorded in one case and in another the information supplied to the pathologist was felt to be inadequate to allow a properly focused postmortem examination.

DISCUSSION AND CONCLUSIONS

This is the first time in a CESDI Enquiry that comparison of babies who died and survivors has been possible. Pathological examination of the placentas from infants at 27–28 weeks gestation showed a range of processes. Perhaps surprisingly, there was no significant difference in the rate of placental ischaemia, infection or abruption between infants who died and those who survived. A greater proportion of survivors' placentas was not examined, and it is possible that those relatively normal placentas were selectively not submitted for examination. Nevertheless, there is a suggestion from these results that the nature of the placental pathology does not provide an indication of whether the baby is likely to survive. However, this study is relatively crude and does not allow correction for the severity of any of these conditions. It also does not look at the relationship between long-term morbidity in survivors and placental pathology. There is, for example, growing evidence to indicate that periventricular leukomalacia is a result of cytokines released in response to amniotic infection (Gilstrap and Ramin, 2000).

In line with numerous previous studies (e.g. Cartlidge et al., 1995; Thornton, 1999), the postmortem examinations performed in this study revealed a substantial amount of unexpected new information. This is despite the many advances in clinical care and investigations. It is difficult to determine the significance of all of these additional findings, in particular whether management would have been different had they been known in life, as the comments are not sufficiently detailed. However, some findings, such as the identification of unsuspected pulmonary hypoplasia and the absence of suspected pulmonary hypoplasia, the absence of clinically suspected congenital heart disease and the identification of unsuspected sepsis or necrotising enterocolitis, are all likely to have been significant. These findings once again highlight the contribution that the information from the postmortem examination can make to clinical audit and education.

Since the Redfern report into events at Alder Hey Hospital (Redfern, 2000) there has been a decline in postmortem examination rates, particularly in infants, including those born prematurely. This study was undertaken before the Redfern report was published but still shows a postmortem examination consent rate of only 36%, reflecting the general decline in autopsy consent rates over recent years.

Panels reported deficiencies in obtaining postmortem examination consent and documenting discussions despite clear evidence of value of autopsies and the requirement to keep records of discussions. The right of parents to be offered postmortem examination, to get as full an explanation of their loss as possible, is as important as their right to refuse.

The data show an association between unsatisfactory postmortem examination reports and examinations performed by non-specialist pathologists. This is most probably due to the lack of experience of many general pathologists in this field and the scarcity of postmortem examinations in many general hospitals. This supports the strong argument for all perinatal autopsies to be performed by specialist perinatal pathologists at regional centres (RCOG/RCP, 2001; RCPCH, 2002). This is probably not achievable in the short term, owing to the severe shortage of qualified staff in this field, but emphasises the need for strategic planning and support for paediatric pathology, for instance via the National Service Frameworks for Maternity and Child Health. Other problems such as excessive delays in postmortem examination and failure to report histology are also probably a reflection of staffing problems. All these problems need addressing so that the value of perinatal pathology is not undermined in the eyes of families and clinicians.

CONCLUSION

Communication is the least tangible aspect of care and, from the point of view of the parents, is one of the most important to manage correctly. Failures were more frequently noted in the care of mothers of babies who died. The two most frequent concerns were poor communication between the maternity and neonatal units within the same hospital and poor communication with the mother before the birth. Setting standards and assessing quality in this area is not easy, but the failures reported in this Enquiry indicate that the topic should be urgently addressed at local and national level. Attention should be given to the manner in which parents are prepared for a premature delivery, together with communication during the time the baby is in intensive care.

More than half of all medical records were considered inadequate, particularly in detail and specifying the plan of care. The lack of standardisation in recording medical events continues to hamper the care of the mother and baby and precludes accurate audit.

RECOMMENDATIONS

Communication

Terms indicated in **bold** are defined in the Glossary (p. xv).

At Trust level

Interdisciplinary communication

15.1 Formal communication should occur at least daily between the obstetric, midwifery and neonatal unit.

15.2 The status and grade of staff within the neonatal service that need to be informed of an anticipated preterm delivery should be determined locally and this information disseminated within the neonatal and maternity units.

15.3 Early communication between the obstetric and neonatal staff should occur to establish the ability of the unit to accept the admission and to agree the optimum timing for delivery.

15.4 The obstetric team should check the availability of neonatal care before accepting an in-utero transfer or delivering a preterm baby. If the unit is unable to accept admission of the baby the senior obstetrician should be informed and if necessary the care of the baby should be diverted to another unit.

15.5 The mother's general practitioner or primary health care team should be informed promptly of the death of a baby, certainly within 24 hours.

Communication with parents

15.6 All women should have a lead midwife who takes responsibility for updating the rest of the team and maintaining effective communication with the mother.

15.7 In circumstances where the delivery is anticipated but not imminent, every effort should be made by the neonatal team to speak to the mother to prepare her for the delivery and the care immediately afterwards.

15.8 All mothers should have the opportunity to discuss the care of their baby with a consultant neonatologist within 24 hours of delivery.

15.9 Parents of infants receiving **intensive care** should be kept informed of progress.

Record-keeping

At national and commissioning level

15.10 Professional organisations should collaborate in the development and implementation of national medical records.

15.11 Commissioners should work with Trusts to introduce common documentation. Priority areas include resuscitation at birth and transfer procedures.

At Trust level

15.12 Departments and Trusts should ensure that their record design conforms to the key features of good record design as specified by the Nursing and Midwifery Council (NMC, 2002).

15.13 Departments and Trusts should consider the benefits of using the same speciality specific records across units.

15.14 Clinicians should conclude each patient contact with an explicit statement of their plan of care. This may be a simple endorsement of a previous plan, or a revision of the plan in the light of changes in condition or a completely new plan.

16 Panel conclusions – overall grade of care

At the end of the review of each case, panels were asked to summarise their view of the overall obstetric and neonatal care. Panel members assessing obstetric care were not aware of the outcome for the baby and were asked to predict whether they thought the baby had lived for more than 28 days. Panel members assessing overall neonatal care were aware of the outcome.

In the first year the panels assessed cases within their own region and in the second year the cases were from a national pool (see Chapter 1). The grades applied by the panels in each year were examined and the distribution of grading was similar for each year. The results are therefore presented for the two years combined.

PANEL OPINION: OVERALL OBSTETRIC CARE

The overall obstetric care was good or acceptable in 61% of babies who died and in 65% of babies who survived (Table 16.1 and Figure 16.1). There was a statistically significant difference in standard of overall obstetric care between the babies who died and those who survived. Major substandard care, in particular, occurred more frequently with the babies who died (Table 16.1).

Table 16.1   Panel opinion: overall obstetric care

	Babies who died (%)[a] n = 366	Babies who survived (%)[a] n = 395	Crude OR (95% CI) p value
Good	113 (31.0)	154 (39.2)	Reference group
Acceptable	108 (29.7)	101 (25.7)	1.46 (1.01–2.10)
Substandard – minor	71 (19.5)	90 (22.9)	1.07 (0.72–1.59)
Substandard – major	72 (19.8)	48 (12.2)	2.04 (1.32–3.17) 0.01[b]
[Data missing]	2	2	

[a]   The percentage was calculated from the number of babies for which the information was provided.
[b]   Test for trend across type of care and its effect on mortality.

Figure 16.1   Grade of overall obstectric care

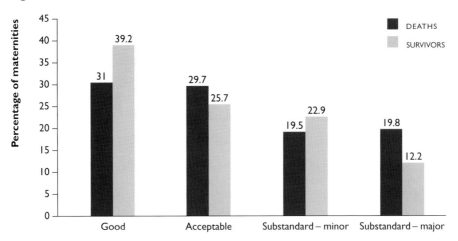

PANEL OPINION: OUTCOME FOR THE BABY

Obstetric assessors were not aware of the outcome for the baby. They were able to predict the outcome correctly in 46% of cases in which the baby died and 83% of cases in which the baby survived (Table 16.2).

Table 16.2   Panel opinion: did the baby live for more than 28 days?

	Babies who died (%)[a] n = 366	Babies who survived (%)[a] n = 395
No	165/357 (46.2)	67/387 (17.3)
Yes	192/357 (53.8)	320/387 (82.7)
[Data missing]	9	8

[a]   The percentage was calculated from the number of babies for which the information was provided.

PANEL OPINION: OVERALL NEONATAL CARE

The overall neonatal care was good or acceptable in 47% of babies who died and in 77% of babies who survived (Table 16.3, Figure 16.2). Because the assessors may have been influenced by the condition of the baby at birth the comparison of care is presented for babies in good condition by 5 minutes of birth (as defined by heart and respiratory rate, see Chapter 2) and for babies in poor condition at 5 minutes. The effect of substandard care was greater in the babies in good condition and this difference was statistically significant (Tables 16.4 and 16.5).

17 *Lost in the figures*

Earlier chapters in the report focus mainly on scientific appraisal. The purpose of the vignettes in this chapter is to link case scenarios with the analysis of the panels' comments in earlier chapters. Specific areas of concern are placed in context of the overall clinical situation.

Learning from adverse events has become a key clinical governance requirement. as set out in *An Organisation with a Memory* (DoH, 2000) and *Building a Safer NHS* (DoH, 2001) Continuing professional development, through participation and review of enquiry reports, supports healthcare professionals in reflecting on their own clinical practice.

Each case reflects the panels' views drawn from a consensus of professional opinion rather than the findings of a formal scientific study. Confidential enquiry panels and the expert opinion of their members may be considered subjective, but their strength is in their multidisciplinary approach. Important practice points can be conveyed in this realistic manner for each healthcare professional within the relevant speciality. Learning the lessons from enquiries can assist in changing practice to reduce risk and recurrence of an adverse outcome at a local level.

Confidentiality concerns have been addressed by making changes to points of detail that do not detract from the overall meaning of the case.

FETAL WELL-BEING – ASSESSMENT PRIOR TO LABOUR (CHAPTER 3)

Deficient investigation

- A 31-year-old woman presented at 15 weeks gestation, with a history of a previous delivery at 30 weeks for IUGR. At 19 weeks, the baby was small for its gestational age and there was reduced liquor volume. It was suggested the dates were wrong and the scan was repeated but showed no change. Scans were done at 23 and 26 weeks confirming IUGR but no further detailed assessments were made. She was seen again at 28 weeks with reduced fetal movements when she was admitted for an emergency caesarean and delivered an infant in poor condition. The baby died in the first week.

- A 33-year-old woman presented with an unplanned pregnancy at 11 weeks gestation, having had two previous births with severe IUGR. At 26 weeks gestation, she had reduced fundal height measurements, and no other assessment was done at this time. At her next visit at 28 weeks, she was admitted for monitoring and required delivery by emergency caesarean section. The baby subsequently died.

ANTENATAL MANAGEMENT OF PRETERM DELIVERY (CHAPTER 4)

Failure to appreciate that steroids were indicated

- A woman presented for booking at 10 weeks gestation. Her past obstetric history showed a miscarriage of twins at 15 weeks gestation. Her booking scan showed she had another twin pregnancy. She was noted to have raised blood pressure at 14 weeks gestation and was started on labetalol 200 mg twice a day. At 27 weeks gestation she presented at the hospital for anti-D at her GP's request because of a small haemorrhage. On the following day, she was seen on the labour ward for a second time with heavier bleeding and lower abdominal pain. She was allowed home the next day after having a normal scan and seeing the SHO. She presented 2 days later with a heavy vaginal bleed and was distressed with abdominal pain. She was fully dilated with intact membranes and delivered 14 hours later. Steroids were not given despite the woman's history of two hospital admissions for bleeding and abdominal pain at 27 weeks gestation.

INTRAPARTUM CARE (CHAPTER 5)

Difficulty in the conduct of deliveries

- A woman had two live children, one delivered by caesarean section and the other a normal delivery. At 18 weeks gestation, she presented with abdominal pain and had a cervical suture inserted because the cervical os was noted to be dilated. She was subsequently admitted at 24 weeks with a history of reduced movements but examination was satisfactory. At 26^{+2} weeks she started to bleed. The suture was removed and she was managed conservatively in the hospital. A week later she transferred to the labour ward with a cord prolapse and a heavy fresh blood loss. She was found to have a compound presentation with a deep head, needing a high incision. The baby was delivered as a breech presentation and there was an accidental incision of the bladder.

- A 41-year-old Afro-Caribbean mother of two presented to her GP at 27 weeks gestation with a blood pressure of 208/112 and gross proteinuria. She was admitted to the labour ward, and after her blood pressure was stabilised she was transferred to another unit with better neonatal facilities. She was seen by the consultant who decided to deliver her immediately because of her worsening condition. The emergency caesarean section was a difficult delivery. The baby was a breech presentation and the uterus had a thick, poorly formed lower segment with multiple fibroids. The incision had to be extended laterally to deliver the head. The baby deteriorated the next day and died.

NEONATAL RESUSCITATION (CHAPTER 6)

Deficiencies in the care given during resuscitation and transfer to the neonatal unit

- A multiparous woman had a rapid normal vaginal delivery at 27 weeks. The baby, weighing 1080 g, was delivered with Apgar scores of 5 at 1 and 5 minutes. It was not possible to identify the healthcare professionals who were present at delivery. The panel were concerned that after birth over 6 minutes elapsed before the baby was intubated, and considered an oxygen saturation level of 50% on arrival to the neonatal unit to indicate sub-standard care. The baby received 7 days of respiratory support and subsequently survived.

- A woman was delivered by emergency caesarean section at 27 weeks due to premature labour chorioamnionitis, and breech presentation. A normally formed baby, weighing 1 kg, was delivered with Apgar scores of 5 at 1 minute, 6 at 5 minutes, and 9 at 15 minutes. A senior house officer and registrar failed on five occasions to intubate. The consultant was called after 10 minutes and on the second attempt correctly placed an endotracheal tube at 25 minutes after birth. The baby died at 6 hours of age, never having achieved adequate ventilation.

EARLY THERMAL CARE (CHAPTER 7)

Baby's temperature failed to meet the standard

- A male infant born at 28 weeks by normal vaginal delivery was intubated at 8 minutes of age. The birth weight was approximately 1 kg and Apgar scores were 3 at 1 minute, 5 at 5 minutes, and 7 at 8 minutes. The baby's temperature on arrival to the neonatal unit was 35°C but fell to 33.4°C, and subsequently took 5 hours to attain 36°C. The notes did not enable the panel members to ascertain the measures taken to regain the temperature, such as when humidification of the incubator was started, or establish the documentation of regular temperature monitoring during procedures.

- A young mother, expecting twins, presented at 27 weeks with spontaneous ruptured membranes in active labour, in a district hospital. Twin 1 was delivered vaginally, but twin 2 was delivered by emergency caesarean section owing to oblique lie. Twin 2 did not have an initial temperature or Apgar score documented. On admission the baby's temperature was 35°C, and he became further hypothermic during the transfer to a tertiary centre. On arrival, there was no documentation of the measures taken to attain the minimum temperature of 36°C, and when it was achieved. Intensive care was withdrawn in the neonatal period following hypotension and uncontrollable respiratory acidosis.

VENTILATORY SUPPORT (CHAPTER 9)

Inability to meet the standard for ventilatory support

- A woman was delivered at 27 weeks gestation by emergency caesarean section because of placental abruption. A baby weighing 1300 g, with Apgar scores of 1 at 1 minute, 2 at 5 minutes, and 6 at 10 minutes, was intubated at 2 minutes of age. The first blood gas was taken at 1 hour after birth. Despite poor results, no remedial action was taken for a further 50 minutes. Subsequent samples also gave cause for concern but there was further delay in taking appropriate action. Severe respiratory distress syndrome required three doses of surfactant, sedation and inotropic support. The baby died as a result of massive pulmonary haemorrhage.

- A multigravid woman was delivered by caesarean section because of worsening twin-to-twin transfusion syndrome. Two doses of

Appendix

Abbreviations

AFP	alphafetoprotein
ANNP	advanced neonatal nurse practitioner
APLS	advanced paediatric life support
BAPM	British Association of Perinatal Medicine
BPA	British Paediatric Association
BPD	bronchopulmonary dysplasia
CESDI	Confidential Enquiry into Stillbirth and Infant Deaths
CI	confidence interval
CPAP	continuous positive airway pressure
CRIB	Clinical Risk Index for Babies
CSAG	Clinical Standards Advisory Group
CTG	cardiotocograph
EFM	electronic fetal monitoring
ETT	endotracheal tube
FHR	fetal heart rate
FMH	feto-maternal hemorrhage
HELLP	haemolysis, elevated liver enzymes, low platelets syndrome
HMD	hyaline membrane disease
IPPV	intermittent positive pressure ventilation
IQR	interquartile range
IVH	intraventricular haemorrhage
IUGR	intrauterine growth retardation
MBP	mean blood pressure (mmHg)
MCHRC	Maternal and Child Health Research Consortium
MRSA	methicillin-resistant *Staphylococcus aureus*

NCPAP	nasal continuous positive airway pressure
NEC	necrotising enterocolitis
NICE	National Institute for Clinical Excellence
NICU	neonatal intensive care unit
NLS	neonatal life support
NMC	Nursing and Midwifery Council
OR	odds ratio
PVH	periventricular haemorrhage
PALS	paediatric advanced life support
PM	postmortem
PROM	prelabour rupture of membranes
RCOG	Royal College of Obstetricians and Gynaecologists
RCPCH	Royal College of Paediatrics and Child Health
RDS	respiratory distress syndrome
SD	standard deviation
SHO	senior house officer
SOGC	Society of Obstetricians and Gynaecologists of Canada
USS	ultrasound scan

Glossary

adjustment The statistical process of controlling for confounding factors at the analysis stage (*see* **confounder**)

aetiology The science of causes, especially of disease

anonymisation Removal of information that would identify babies, family members, professionals or institutions

antepartum stillbirth Death of a baby before the onset of labour

bias Any effect at any stage of investigation that tends to cause results to depart systematically from the true values. Examples include observer bias due to differences among observers recording study results; and selection bias, where systematic differences occur between selection of cases and controls

biophysical profile A process of monitoring changes in fetal well-being which provides indirect information about fetal neurological and neuromuscular function. This includes creating a score and considering the significance of measurements of fetal movement, tone, reactivity, breathing and amniotic fluid volume

cardiotocography Electronic monitoring of the fetal heart rate and of uterine contractions. The fetal heart rate is recorded by means of either an external ultrasonic abdominal transducer or a fetal scalp electrode. Uterine contractions are recorded by means of an abdominal pressure transducer. The recordings are graphically represented on a continuous paper printout (trace)

case control studies Studies that compare exposures in people who have a particular disease or outcome with those who do not

chorioamnionitis	Acute clinical infection of the amniotic fluid and intrauterine contents
confidence interval	A range of values for which there is a 95% chance that it includes the true value. For example, if the stillbirth rate is 5.4 per 1000 total births and the 95% confidence intervals are 5.3–5.5 per 1000 total births, then there is a 95% chance that the actual stillbirth rate lies between 5.3 and 5.5 per 1000 total births
Confidential Enquiry	Enquiry by peer groups, including experts in the field, into the cause of, and the factors surrounding, a death where strict confidentiality is observed at all stages of the process. It is a form of clinical audit, with an important difference that the feedback or 'closing of the audit loop' is via reports on the general findings, and not by direct feedback to those involved with the individual cases subjected to enquiry
confidentiality	Information given in confidence may be used only for the purposes for which it is given. There are legal and ethical duties to maintain confidentiality in the NHS. The principles on which CESDI data are collected are that the identities of the panels, the professionals involved, and the mothers and families of the babies that died will be anonymous within the enquiry. As a result it is not possible to release panel reports to outside agencies on any identifiable or individualised basis
confounder	A factor that can bring an alternative explanation to an association observed between an exposure (e.g. standards of care) and the outcome of interest (e.g. death)
congenital malformation/ anomaly	A physical malformation (including biochemical abnormality) which is present at birth
control	In a case control study or randomized controlled trial, a control is a person in a comparison group that differs only in their experience of the disease in question. If matched controls are used they are selected so that they are similar to the study group, or cases, in specific characteristics (e.g. age, sex, weight)

denominators	The population at risk in the calculation of a rate or ratio. Examples relevant to CESDI include number of all live births as a denominator for neonatal mortality rate, or birthweight distribution of all live births for birthweight-specific mortality calculations
early neonatal death	Death during the first week of life (0–6 completed days inclusive)
enquiry	*see* **Confidential Enquiry**

equipment

Each neonatal intensive care and high dependency cot should have available the following equipment available (BAPM, 2001):

- incubator or unit with radiant heating
- ventilator (for intensive care cot only) and NCPAP driver with humidifier
- syringe/infusion pumps
- facilities for monitoring the following variables:
  - respiration
  - heart rate
  - intravascular blood pressure
  - transcutaneous or intra-arterial oxygen tension
  - oxygen saturation
  - ambient oxygen

fetal death	Death before complete expulsion or extraction from its mother of a recognizable fetus, irrespective of duration of pregnancy. After separation, the fetus does not show any evidence of life. (Based on WHO recommended definition.)
gestation	The time from conception to birth. The duration of gestation is measured from the first day of the last normal menstrual period.

high-dependency care

Criteria for receipt of high-dependency care (BAPM, 2001) are:

- receiving NCPAP for any part of the day but not fulfilling any of the criteria for intensive care
- below 1000 g current weight and not fulfilling any of the criteria for intensive care

- receiving parenteral nutrition
- having convulsions
- receiving oxygen therapy and below 1500 g current weight
- requiring treatment for neonatal abstinence syndrome
- requiring specified procedures that do not fulfil any criteria for intensive care:
  - care of an intra-arterial catheter or chest drain
  - partial exchange transfusion
  - tracheostomy care until supervised by a parent
  - requiring frequent stimulation for severe apnoea

inappropriate transfer

The Clinical Standards Advisory Group has identified two types of poor practice:

- Mothers and infants should not be forced to travel beyond their nearest referral centre (or centres if they are more or less equidistant)
- Tertiary centres should not transfer out their own high-risk mothers and infants.

This definition was used in the national census of availability of neonatal intensive care

infant death

Death in the first year following live birth; on or before the 365th day of life (366th in a leap year)

infant mortality rate *see* **mortality rates**

intensive care

Criteria for receipt of intensive care (BAPM, 2001) are:

- receiving any respiratory support via a tracheal tube and in the first 24 hours after its withdrawal
- receiving NCPAP for any part of the day and less than 5 days old
- below 1000 g current weight and receiving NCPAP for any part of the day and for 24 hours after withdrawal
- less than 29 weeks gestational age and less than 48 hours old

- requiring major emergency surgery, for the preoperative period and postoperatively for 24 hours
- requiring complex clinical procedures:
  - full exchange transfusion
  - peritoneal dialysis
  - infusion of an inotrope, pulmonary vasodilator or prostaglandin and for 24 hours afterwards
- any other very unstable baby considered by the nurse-in-charge to need 1 : 1 nursing
- a baby on the day of death.

interquartile range The spread of a set of values between which 25% (25th centile) and 75% (75th centile) of these values lie

intrapartum death Intrapartum means during labour, between the onset of (effective) contractions and ending with completion of delivery of the baby. If a baby is born without signs of life, but also without maceration (the skin and other changes that occur a varying length of time after death in the womb), there is a strong presumption that death occurred during labour. There are exceptions in both directions, which require judgment on the timing of death in relation to the presumed onset of labour

late fetal loss For CESDI, a late fetal loss is defined as a death occurring between 20 weeks + 0 days and 23 weeks + 6 days. If gestation is not known or not sure, all births of at least 300 g are reported. Late fetal loss and stillbirth are distinguished by gestational age at the time of delivery, which is not necessarily the time of death

live birth Delivery of an infant, which after complete separation from its mother, shows any signs of life. There is no recognized gestation or weight qualifier in UK law on birth registration, so that any birth, at any gestation or birthweight, that fulfils these criteria, should be registered as a live birth

mortality rates	• **Infant mortality rate:** deaths under the age of 1 year following live birth, per 1000 live births
	• **Perinatal mortality rate:** the number of stillbirths and early neonatal deaths (those occurring in the first week of life) per 1000 live and stillbirths
	• **Neonatal death rate:** the number of neonatal deaths (i.e. occurring within the first 28 days of life) per 1000 live births
	• **Postneonatal mortality rate:** the number of infants who die between 28 days and less than 1 year per 1000 live births
	• **Stillbirth rate:** the number of stillbirths per 1000 total births (live births and stillbirths)
	• **Late fetal loss rate:** the number of late fetal losses per 1000 of total births (live births and stillbirths)
neonatal care	Standard categories for hospitals providing neonatal intensive and high dependency care have been defined by the British Association of Perinatal Medicine (BAPM, 2001). *See* **intensive care; high dependency care; special care; normal care**
neonatal death	Death before the age of 28 completed days
non-registrable death	A fetus delivered before the end of 24 completed weeks of pregnancy without signs of life
normal care	Care provided for babies who themselves have no medical indication to be in an intensive care unit in hospital (BAPM, 2001)
notification of birth	By law all births must be notified to the District Medical Officer (now Director of Public Health) in England and Wales and the Chief Administrative Medical Officer in Scotland and Northern Ireland within 36 hours of their occurrence
odds ratio	A measure of the excess risk or degree of protection given by exposure to a certain factor. An odds ratio of greater than 1 shows an increased risk and less than 1 shows a protective effect

perinatal death	Fetal deaths after 24 completed weeks gestation and death before 6 completed days
perinatal mortality rate *see* **mortality rates**	
postneonatal infant death	Death between 1 month and 1 year of age (28 days and over, up to 1 year)
postneonatal mortality rate *see* **mortality rates**	
registration of birth	A statutory requirement for all births in England, Wales and Northern Ireland within 42 days
registration of death	Time limit for registration in England, Wales and Northern Ireland is 5 days
special care	Care provided for all babies not receiving intensive or high dependency care but whose carers could not reasonably be expected to look after them in hospital or at home (BAPM, 2001)
stillbirth	Legal definitions:

- England and Wales: A child that has issued forth from its mother after the 24th week of pregnancy and which did not at any time after being completely expelled from its mother breathe or show any other signs of life.

- Northern Ireland: A stillbirth 'means the complete expulsion from its mother after the 24th week of pregnancy of a child which did not at anytime after being completely expelled or extracted breathe or show any other evidence of life'.

tocolysis	The process of suppressing uterine contractions in preterm labour with beta-mimetic drugs (e.g. ritrodrine)

Project 27/28   CESDI Standards Document

> **Standards are classified, according to the scheme endorsed by the NHS Executive to show the level of evidence on which they are based**
>
> Grade A: Evidence from randomised controlled trials
> Grade B: Evidence from other robust experimental or observational studies
> Grade C: More limited evidence, but the standard relies on expert opinion and has the endorsement of respected authorities

Standards for Obstetric care

Antenatal administration of Steroids
Every effort should be made to treat women with a course of steroids prior to pre-term delivery.[1,2] (A course consists of betamethasone 24mg or dexamethasone 24mg in divided doses)

Category of evidence
A

Standards for Neonatal care

Resuscitation

Category of evidence

Personnel present for resuscitation Intermediate grade paediatric staff and/or a consultant neonatal paediatrician, in addition to a junior paediatrician from the neonatal unit, should be present for the delivery[3]

C

In the first minute after birth If there are absent or ineffective respirations or persistent heart rate of <100 beats/min, then IPPV should be administered via a bag and mask or tracheal intubation without delay[4]

C

5 minutes after birth If there are absent or ineffective respirations or persistent heart rate of <100 beats/minute, then IPPV should be administered via a tracheal tube[7]

C

At any time during resuscitation After effective IPPV has been established, if at any age the heart rate is <60 beats/minute external chest compression should be performed.[4]

C

On admission to the neonatal unit If there are absent or ineffective respirations or persistent heart rate of <100 beats/minute, then mechanical ventilation should be administered via a tracheal tube (in some cases CPAP may be appropriate)[7]

C

Standards for Neonatal care

	Category of evidence
Early thermal care	
The infant's temperature on admission to the neonatal unit should be above 36°C.[5]	C
Surfactant therapy	
Surfactant should be administered to all intubated infants[6]	A
Surfactant should be administered as soon as practical after birth [8]	A
Ventilatory support	
Regular blood gas analysis should be performed whilst the infant remains ventilated, on CPAP or in supplementary oxygen. [5]	C
Ventilation should be adjusted with the *aim* of maintaining a pH >7.25 and PaO_2 6-10kPa. [5]	C
The response to therapy should be clearly recorded along with the remedial action taken.[7]	C
Cardio-vascular support	
Blood pressure should be monitored regularly whilst the infant remains unwell. [5]	C
The mean blood pressure (mmHg) should be managed with the aim of maintaining it at or above the infant's gestation in weeks.[5]	C
The response to therapy should be clearly recorded along with any remedial action taken.[7]	C

References

1. Crowley P. Corticosteroids prior to preterm delivery. The Cochrane Library, Issue 2. Oxford: Update Software; 1998
2. RCOG Guideline No 7, 1996
3. British Paediatric Association. Neonatal Resuscitation. London: The British Paediatric Association 1993.
4. Resuscitation of Babies at Birth. Royal College of Paediatrics and Child Health and Royal College of Obstetricians and Gynaecologists. BMJ Publishing Group, 1997.
5. Report of a Working Group of the British Association of Perinatal Medicine and the Research Unit of the Royal College of Physicians. Development of audit measures and guidelines for good practice in the management of neonatal respiratory distress syndrome. 1992 Archives of Disease in Childhood; 67: 1221-1227.
6. Soll RF, Morley CJ. Prophylactic surfactant vs treatment with surfactant. (Cochrane Review) In: The Cochrane Library, Issue 2. Oxford: Update Software; 1998. Updated quarterly.
7. Project 27/28 Working Group. Confidential Enquiry into Stillbirths and Deaths in Infancy, 1998.
8. British Association of Perinatal Medicine. Guidelines for good practice in the management of neonatal respiratory distress syndrome. (To be published)

This document was produced under the direction of the Paediatric Working Group of CESDI as an educational aid to health professionals. The standard is not intended to dictate an exclusive course of management. Variations of practice taking into account the needs of the individual patient, resources and limitations unique to the institution or type of practice may be appropriate.

References

Aghajafari F, Murphy K, Willan A, Ohlsson A, Arnankwah K, Matthews S, Hannah M (2001) Multiple courses of antenatal corticosteroids: a systematic review and meta-analysis. *American Journal of Obstetrics and Gynecology* **185**: 1073–1080.

Ainsworth SB, Beresford MW, Milligan DWA, Shaw NJ, Matthews JNS, Fenton AC, Ward Platt MP (2000) Pumactant and poractant alfa for treatment of respiratory distress syndrome in neonates born at 25–29 weeks gestation: a randomised trial. *Lancet* **355**: 1387–1392.

All Wales Perinatal Survey and CESDI (1997 and 1999). Cardiff: Perinatal Survey Office, University of Wales College of Medicine.

BAPM (1999) *Guidelines for the Management of Respiratory Distress Syndrome*, London: British Association of Perinatal Medicine.

BAPM (2001) *Standards for Hospitals Providing Neonatal Intensive and High Dependency Care* (1st edn 1996), London: British Association of Perinatal Medicine.

BAPM/RCPCH (1992) Report of a Joint Working Group of the British Association of Perinatal Medicine and the Research Unit of the Royal College of Paediatrics and Child Health. Development of audit measures and guidelines for good practice in the management of neonatal respiratory distress syndrome. *Archives of Disease in Childhood* **67**: 1221–1227.

BPA (1993) *Neonatal Resuscitation*. London: The British Paediatric Association.

Bruck K (1992) Neonatal thermoregulation. In: Polin R, Fox WW, eds. *Fetal and Neonatal Physiology*, Philadelphia: WB Saunders, pp. 488–515.

Cartlidge PHT, Dawson AJ, Stewart JH, Vujanic GM (1995) Value and quality of perinatal and infant postmortem examinations: cohort analysis of 400 consecutive deaths. *BMJ* **310**: 155–158.

CEMD (2001) *Why Mothers Die. 50th Report of the Confidential Enquiry into Maternal Deaths*, London: Maternal and Child Health Consortium.

CESDI (1996) *Confidential Enquiry into Stillbirths and Deaths in Infancy: 3rd Annual Report, 1 January–31 December 1994*, London: Maternal and Child Health Research Consortium.

CESDI (1999) *Confidential Enquiry into Stillbirths and Deaths in Infancy: 6th Annual Report, 1 January–31 December 1997*, London: Maternal and Child Health Research Consortium.

CESDI (2000) *Confidential Enquiry into Stillbirths and Deaths in Infancy: 7th Annual Report, 1 January–31 December 1998*, London: Maternal and Child Health Research Consortium.

CESDI (2001) *Confidential Enquiry into Stillbirths and Deaths in Infancy: 8th Annual Report, 1 January–31 December 1999*. London: Maternal and Child Health Research Consortium.

Chapple J (2001) Perinatal mortality In: Chamberlain G, Steer P, eds. *Turnbull's Obstetrics* (3rd edn), Edinburgh: Churchill Livingstone, Chapter 47, pp. 729–741.

CSAG (1993) *Access and Availability of Neonatal Intensive Care*, London: HMSO.

Crowley P (1998) Corticosteroids prior to preterm delivery. *Cochrane Library*, Issue 2, Oxford: Update Software.

Crowley P (2002) Prophylactic corticosteroids for preterm birth. *Cochrane Library*, Issue 1, Oxford: Update Software.

Curley AE, Halliday HL (2001) The present status of exogenous surfactant for the newborn. *Early Human Development* **61**: 67–83.

Dammann O, Allred EN, Kuban KC, van Marter LJ, Stewart JE, Pagano M, Leviton A (2001) Hypocarbia during the first 24 postnatal hours and white matter echolucencies in newborns ≤ 28 weeks gestation. *Pediatric Research* **49**(3): 388–393.

Dear P (1999) Neonatal infection. In: Rennie JM, Roberton NRC, eds, *Textbook of Neonatology*, 3rd edn, Edinburgh: Churchill Livingstone.

DoH (2000) *An Organisation with a Memory*, London: Department of Health.

DoH (2001) *Building a Safer NHS for Patients*, London: Department of Health.

Egan G (2002) Reluctant and resistant clients. In: *The Skilled Helper: A Problem-Management and Opportunity-Development Approach to Helping* (7th edn), Pacific Grove, CA: Brookes/Cole, pp. 162–173.

Egberts J, Brand R, Walti H, Bevilacqua G, Breart G, Gardini F (1997) Mortality, severe respiratory distress syndrome and chronic lung disease of the newborn are reduced more after prophylactic than after therapeutic administration of the surfactant curosurf. *Pediatrics* **100**(1).

Ewer AK, Tyler W, Francis A, Drinkall D, Gardosi JO (in press) Excessive volume expansion and neonatal death in preterm infants born at 27–28 weeks gestation. *Pediatric and Perinatal Epidemiology*.

Ferlie E, Pettigrew (1996) Managing through networks: some issues and implications for the NHS. *British Journal of Management* **7**, special issue: S81–S99.

Field D (1999) Organisation of perinatal care. In: Rennie JM, Roberton NRC, eds, *Textbook of Neonatology*, 3rd edn, Edinburgh: Churchill Livingstone.

Field D, Hodges S, Mason P, Burton P (1991) Survival and place of treatment after premature delivery. *Archives of Disease in Childhood* **66**: 408–411.

Gilstrap LC 3rd, Ramin SM (2000) Infection and cerebral palsy. *Seminars in Perinatology* **24**: 200–203.

Grauel EL, Halle E, Bollmann R, Buchholz P, Buttenberg S (1989) Neonatal septicaemia – incidence, etiology and outcome. *Acta Paediatric Scandinavica Supplement* **360**: 113–119.

Gunn AJ, Bennet L (2001) Is temperature important in delivery room resuscitation? *Seminars in Neonatology* **6**: 241–249.

Hall M, Ironton R (1999) Infection. In: Levitt G, Harvey D, Cooke R, eds, *Practical Perinatal Care: The Baby Under 1000 g*, Oxford: Butterworth Heinemann.

Halperin ME, Moore DC, Hannah WJ. (1988) Classical versus low-segment transverse incision for preterm caesarean section: maternal complications and outcome of subsequent pregnancies. *British Journal of Obstetrics and Gynaecology* **95**(10): 990–996.

Health Service Ombudsman (2002) *Investigations Completed December 2001 – March 2002. Part 1 – Summaries of Investigations Completed.* HC 924–1 (www.ombudsman.org.uk).

Holdcroft A (2000) Monitoring of mother and fetus before and during regional analgesia. In: Lack JA, White LA, Thoms GM, Rollin A-M, eds, *Raising the Standard*, London: Royal College of Anaesthetists.

Holdcroft A, Thomas TA (2000) Anaesthesia for Caesarean Section. In: *Principles and Practice of Obstetric Anaesthesia and Analgesia*, Oxford: Blackwell Science Ltd, p. 285.

IFS (2002) *Infant Feeding Survey 2000*, London: The Stationery Office.

International Neonatal Network (1993) The CRIB (clinical risk index for babies) score: a tool for assessing initial neonatal risk and comparing performance of neonatal intensive care units. *Lancet* **342**: 193–198.

Kattwinkel J, Niermeyer S, Nadkarni V, Tibballs J, Phillips B, Zideman D, Van Reempts P, Osmond M (1999) Resuscitation of the newly born infant: an advisory statement from the Pediatric Working Group of the International Liaison Committee on Resuscitation. *Resuscitation* **40**(2): 71–88.

Kendig JW, Cox C, Maniscalo WM, Sinkin RA, Reubens L, Horgan MJ, Dweck HS, Phelps DL and the Rochester surfactant study group. (1996) Surfactant prophylaxis as immediate bolus (IB) versus post-ventilatory aliquots (PVA): A multicenter randomised trial. *Pediatrics Research* **39**(4): 221A.

Kenyon S, Boulvain M, Neilson J (2002) Antibiotics for preterm premature rupture of membranes (Cochrane Review). *Cochrane Library*, Issue 1, Oxford: Update Software.

Lancaster T, Stead L, Silagy C, Sowden A. (2000) Effectiveness of intervention to help people stop smoking: findings from the Cochrane Library. *BMJ* **321**:355–358.

Leslie AJ, Stephenson TJ (1997) Audit of neonatal intensive care transport – closing the loop. *Acta Paediatrica* **86**(11):1253–1256.

Lewis DF, Major CA, Towers CV et al. (1992) Effects of digital vaginal examinations on latency period in preterm premature rupture of membranes. *Obstetrics and Gynaecology* **80** (4): 630–634.

Lieberman E, Lang J, Richardson DK, Frigoletto FD, Heffner LJ, Cohen A (2000) Intrapartum maternal fever and neonatal outcome. *Pediatrics* **105**: 8–13

Low JA, Panagiotopoulos C, Smith JT, Tang W, Derrick EJ (1995) Validity of newborn oscillometric blood pressure. *Clinical and Investigative Medicine* **18**(3):163–167.

Macfarlane A, Mugford M (2000) *Birth Counts: Statistics of Pregnancy and Childbirth*, London, The Stationery Office, p. 181.

Malathi I, Millar MR, Leeming JP, Hedges A, Marlow N (1993) Skin disinfection in preterm infants. *Archives of Disease in Childhood* **69**(3, special number): 312–316.

Mok Q, Bass CA, Ducker DA, McIntosh N (1991) Temperature instability during nursing procedures in preterm neonates. *Archives of Disease in Childhood* **66**: 783–786.

Morgan BM, Magni V and Goroszeniuk T (1990) Anaesthesia for emergency caesarean section. *British Journal of Obstetrics and Gynaecology* **97**: 420-424.

Neilson JP, Alfirevic Z (2002) Doppler ultrasound for fetal assessment in high risk pregnancies. *Cochrane Review*, Issue 1, Oxford: Update Software.

NMC (2002) *Guidelines for Records and Record-keeping*, London: Nursing and Midwifery Council.

O'Shea TM, Klinepeter KL, Dillard RG (1998) Prenatal events and the risk of cerebral palsy in very low birth weight infants. *American Journal of Epidemiology* **147**(4): 362–369.

Osborn DA, Evans N (2001) Early volume expansion for prevention of morbidity and mortality in very preterm infants (Cochrane Review). *Cochrane Library*, Issue 2, Oxford: Update Software.

Osiris Collaborative Group (1992) Early versus delayed neonatal administration of a synthetic surfactant: the judgment of OSIRIS. *Lancet* **340**: 1363–1369.

Parmanum J, Field D, Rennie J, Steer P on behalf of the BAPM (2000) National census of availability of neonatal intensive care. *BMJ* **321**: 727–729.

Patel D, Piotrowski ZH (2002) Positive changes among very low birth weight infant Apgar scores that are associated with the neonatal resuscitation program in Illinois. *Journal of Perinatology* **22**: 386–390.

RCOG (1997) *Beta-agonists for the Care of Women in Preterm Labour*. Guideline No. 1(A), London: Royal College of Obstetricians and Gynaecologists.

RCOG (1999) *Antenatal Corticosteroids to Prevent Respiratory Distress Syndrome*. Guideline No. 7, London: Royal College of Obstetricians and Gynaecologists.

RCOG (2000) *Continuing Professional Development*. Report of a Working Party, London: Royal College of Obstetricians and Gynaecologists.

RCOG (2002) *The Management of Breech Presentation*. Guideline No. 20, London: Royal College of Obstetricians and Gynaecologists.

RCOG (in preparation) *Tocolytic Drugs for Women in Preterm Labour*. Guideline No. 1(B), London: Royal College of Obstetricians and Gynaecologists.

RCOG/RCM (1999) *Towards Safer Childbirth: Minimum Standards for the Organisation of Labour Wards*. Report of a Joint Working Party, London: Royal College of Obstetricians and Gynaecologists and Royal College of Midwives.

RCOG/RCP (2001) *Fetal and Perinatal Pathology*. Report of a joint working party, London: Royal College of Obstetricians and Gynaecologists and Royal College of Physicians.

RCPCH (2000) *Guidelines for Good Practice. Management of Neonatal Respiratory Distress Syndrome*, London: Royal College of Paediatrics and Child Health.

RCPCH (2002) *Fetal, Perinatal and Paediatric Pathology: A Critical Future*. Joint Royal Colleges Working Group, London: Royal College of Paediatrics and Child Health.

RCPCH (1995) *Neonatal Intensive Care: Access to and Availability of Specialist Services*. Second report to Clinical Standards Advisory Group by a working group, London: Royal College of Paediatrics and Child Health.

RCPCH/RCOG (1997) *Resuscitation of Babies at Birth*. Royal College of Paediatrics and Child Health and Royal College of Obstetricians and Gynaecologists, London: BMJ Publishing Group.

Redfern M (2000) *The Royal Liverpool Children's Hospital Inquiry*, London: HMSO.

Romero R, Oyarzun E, Mazor M, Sirtori M, Hobbins JC, Bracken M (1989) Meta-analysis of the relationship between asymptomatic bacteriuria and preterm delivery/low birth weight. *Obstetrics and Gynecology* 73(4): 576–782.

Silverman W, Fertig J, Berger A (1958) The incidence of thermal environment upon the survival of newly born premature infants. *Pediatrics* 22: 876–886.

Sinclair JC (2001) Servo-control for maintaining abdominal skin temperature at 36°C in low birthweight infants (Cochrane Review). *Cochrane Library*, Issue 1, Oxford: Update Software.

Smith SL, Hall MA (in press) Developing a neonatal workforce – role evolution and retention of advanced neonatal nursing practitioners. *Archives of Disease in Childhood*, to appear.

SOGC (2002) *Preterm Birth: Making a Difference*. Clinical Practice Guidelines, Society of Obstetricians and Gynaecologists of Canada (http://www.sogc.org).

Soll RF (1998) Prophylactic administration of natural surfactant (Cochrane Review). *Cochrane Library*, Oxford: Update Software.

Soll RF (2001) Multiple versus single dose natural surfactant extract for severe neonatal respiratory distress syndrome (Cochrane Review). Cochrane Library, Issue 2, Oxford: Update Software.

Soll RF, Blanco F (2001) Natural surfactant extract versus synthetic surfactant for neonatal respiratory distress syndrome (Cochrane Review). *Cochrane Library*, Issue 2, Oxford: Update Software.

Soll RF, Morley CJ (1998) Prophylactic surfactant vs. treatment with surfactant (Cochrane Review). *Cochrane Library*, Issue 2, Oxford: Update Software.

Soll RF, Morley CJ (2001) Prophylactic versus selective use of surfactant for preventing mordidity and mortality in preterm infants (Cochrane Review). *Cochrane Library*, Issue 1, Oxford: Update Software.

Subhedar NV, Shaw NJ (2001) Dopamine versus dobutamine for hypotensive preterm infants (Cochrane Review). *Cochrane Library*, Issue 2, Oxford: Update Software.

Tarnow-Mordi W, Parry G, McCabe C, Nicolson P, Tucker J on behalf of the UK Neonatal Staffing Study Group (2000) *Risk Adjusted Outcomes, Patient Volume and Staffing Provision in a Stratified Random Sample of All UK Neonatal Intensive Care Units*. Final Report, NHS National R&D Programme: Mother and Child Health, NHS Executive South East.

Thornton CM (1999) Perinatal pathology. Chapter 5 in: *Confidential Enquiry into Stillbirths and Deaths in Infancy. 6th Annual Report*, London: Maternal and Child Health Research Consortium

Tucker J (2002) Patient volume, staffing, and workload in relation to risk-adjusted outcomes in a random stratified sample of UK neonatal intensive care units: a prospective evaluation. *Lancet* 359(9301): 99–107.

Van Reempts P, Kegalaers B, Van Dam K, Van Overmeire B (1993) Neonatal outcome after very prolonged and premature rupture of membranes. *American Journal of Perinatology* 10(4): 288–291.

Vermont-Oxford (1993) The investigators of the Vermont-Oxford trials network database project. The Vermont-Oxford trials network: very low birth weight outcomes for 1990. *Pediatrics* **91**: 540–545.

Versmold HT, Kitterman JA, Phibbs RH, Gregory GA, Tooley WH (1981) Aortic blood pressure during the first 12 hours of life in infants with birth weight 610 to 4,220 grams. *Pediatrics* **67**(5): 607–613.

Vohra S, Frent G, Campbell V, Abbott M, Whyte R (1999) Effect of polyethylene occlusive skin wrapping on heat loss in very low birth weight infants at delivery: a randomised trial. *Journal of Pediatrics* **134**: 547–551.

Weindling AM, Kissack CM (2001) Blood pressure and tissue oxygenation in the newborn baby at risk of brain damage. *Biology of the Neonate* **79**(3–4): 241–245.

WHO (1997) *Thermal Protection of the Newborn*, WHO/RHT/MSM/97.2, Geneva, World Health Organization.

Wigglesworth JS, Desai R, Guerrini P (1981) Fetal lung hypoplasia: biochemical and structural variations and their possible significance. *Archives of Disease in Childhood* **56**: 606–615.

Wu YW, Colford Jr JM (2000) Chorioamnionitis as a risk factor for cerebral palsy: a meta-analysis *JAMA* **284**: 2996–2997.